Stylistics

Peter Verdonk is Professor of Stylistics
at the University of Amsterdam

D0187694

Published in this series:

Oxford Introductions to Language Study

Series Editor H.G. Widdowson

Stylistics

Peter Verdonk

OXFORD

UNIVERSITY PRESS

OXFORD
UNIVERSITY PRESS

Great Clarendon Street, Oxford OX2 6DP

Oxford University Press is a department of the University
of Oxford. It furthers the University's objective of excellence
in research, scholarship, and education by publishing
worldwide in

Oxford   New York

Athens   Auckland   Bangkok   Bogotá   Buenos Aires
Calcutta   Cape Town   Chennai   Dar es Salaam   Delhi
Florence   Hong Kong   Istanbul   Karachi   Kolkuta
Kuala Lumpur   Madrid   Melbourne   Mexico City
Mumbai   Nairobi   Paris   São Paulo   Shanghai
Singapore   Taipei   Tokyo   Toronto   Warsaw

with associated companies in
Berlin   Ibadan

OXFORD and OXFORD ENGLISH are registered trade marks of
Oxford University Press in the UK and in certain other countries

© Oxford University Press 2002
The moral rights of the author have been asserted
Database right Oxford University Press (maker)
First published 2002

No unauthorized photocopying

All rights reserved. No part of this publication may be
reproduced, stored in a retrieval system, or transmitted, in any
form or by any means, without the prior permission in writing
of Oxford University Press, or as expressly permitted by law,
or under terms agreed with the appropriate reprographics
rights organization. Enquiries concerning reproduction outside
the scope of the above should be sent to the ELT Rights
Department, Oxford University Press, at the address above

You must not circulate this book in any other binding or cover
and you must impose this same condition on any acquirer

ISBN 0 19 437240 5

Typeset by G. M. Brasnett, Cambridge
in Adobe Sabon & ITC Franklin Gothic

Printed in Spain by Unigraf S.L.

for j

Contents

Preface

Purpose

What justification might there be for a series of introductions to language study? After all, linguistics is already well served with introductory texts: expositions and explanations which are comprehensive, authoritative, and excellent in their way. Generally speaking, however, their way is the essentially academic one of providing a detailed initiation into the discipline of linguistics, and they tend to be lengthy and technical: appropriately so, given their purpose. But they can be quite daunting to the novice. There is also a need for a more general and gradual introduction to language: transitional texts which will ease people into an understanding of complex ideas. This series of introductions is designed to serve this need.

Their purpose, therefore, is not to supplant but to support the more academically oriented introductions to linguistics: to prepare the conceptual ground. They are based on the belief that it is an advantage to have a broad map of the terrain sketched out before one considers its more specific features on a smaller scale, a general context in reference to which the detail makes sense. It is sometimes the case that students are introduced to detail without it being made clear what it is a detail *of*. Clearly, a general understanding of ideas is not sufficient: there needs to be closer scrutiny. But equally, close scrutiny can be myopic and meaningless unless it is related to the larger view. Indeed, it can be said that the precondition of more particular enquiry is an awareness of what, in general, the particulars are about. This series is designed to provide this large-scale view of different areas of language study. As such it can serve as a preliminary to (and precondition for) the more specific and specialized enquiry which students of linguistics are required to undertake.

But the series is not only intended to be helpful to such students. There are many people who take an interest in language without being academically engaged in linguistics *per se*. Such people may recognize the importance of understanding language for their own lines of enquiry, or for their own practical purposes, or quite simply for making them aware of something which figures so centrally in their everyday lives. If linguistics has revealing and relevant things to say about language, this should presumably not be a privileged revelation, but one accessible to people other than linguists. These books have been so designed as to accommodate these broader interests too: they are meant to be introductions to language more generally as well as to linguistics as a discipline.

Design

The books in the series are all cut to the same basic pattern. There are four parts: Survey, Readings, References, and Glossary.

Survey

This is a summary overview of the main features of the area of language study concerned: its scope and principles of enquiry, its basic concerns and key concepts. These are expressed and explained in ways which are intended to make them as accessible as possible to people who have no prior knowledge or expertise in the subject. The Survey is written to be readable and is uncluttered by the customary scholarly references. In this sense, it is simple. But it is not simplistic. Lack of specialist expertise does not imply an inability to understand or evaluate ideas. Ignorance means lack of knowledge, not lack of intelligence. The Survey, therefore, is meant to be challenging. It draws a map of the subject area in such a way as to stimulate thought and to invite a critical participation in the exploration of ideas. This kind of conceptual cartography has its dangers of course: the selection of what is significant, and the manner of its representation, will not be to the liking of everybody, particularly not, perhaps, to some of those inside the discipline. But these surveys are written in the belief that there must be an alternative to a technical account on the one hand and an idiot's guide on the other if linguistics is to be made relevant to people in the wider world.

Readings

Some people will be content to read, and perhaps re-read, the summary Survey. Others will want to pursue the subject and so will use the Survey as the preliminary for more detailed study. The Readings provide the necessary transition. For here the reader is presented with texts extracted from the specialist literature. The purpose of these Readings is quite different from the Survey. It is to get readers to focus on the specifics of what is said, and how it is said, in these source texts. Questions are provided to further this purpose: they are designed to direct attention to points in each text, how they compare across texts, and how they deal with the issues discussed in the Survey. The idea is to give readers an initial familiarity with the more specialist idiom of the linguistics literature, where the issues might not be so readily accessible, and to encourage them into close critical reading.

References

One way of moving into more detailed study is through the Readings. Another is through the annotated References in the third section of each book. Here there is a selection of works (books and articles) for further reading. Accompanying comments indicate how these deal in more detail with the issues discussed in the different chapters of the Survey.

Glossary

Certain terms in the Survey appear in bold. These are terms used in a special or technical sense in the discipline. Their meanings are made clear in the discussion, but they are also explained in the Glossary at the end of each book. The Glossary is cross-referenced to the Survey, and therefore serves at the same time as an index. This enables readers to locate the term and what it signifies in the more general discussion, thereby, in effect, using the Survey as a summary work of reference.

Use

The series has been designed so as to be flexible in use. Each title is separate and self-contained, with only the basic format in common. The four sections of the format, as described here, can be drawn upon and combined in different ways, as required by the needs, or interests, of different readers. Some may be content with the Survey and the Glossary and may not want to follow up the suggested References. Some may not wish to venture into the Readings. Again, the Survey might be considered as appropriate preliminary reading for a course in applied linguistics or teacher education, and the Readings more appropriate for seminar discussion during the course. In short, the notion of an introduction will mean different things to different people, but in all cases the concern is to provide access to specialist knowledge and stimulate an awareness of its significance. This series as a whole has been designed to provide this access and promote this awareness in respect to different areas of language study.

H.G. WIDDOWSON

Author's Preface

Because the Series Editor's Preface contains a lucid explanation of the purpose, design, and use of the *Oxford Introductions to Language Study*, I shall restrict myself here to some personal observations about the writing of this book in the series.

First, Henry Widdowson's carefully thought-out editorial brief proved a reliable compass when I tried to 'draw a conceptual map', as he put it, of the well-trodden field of stylistics. Obviously, given the book's modest size, I had to be selective in my choice of topics, and to deal with them in such a way that the reader would see them as distinctive elements of a developing exposition of the central issues in stylistic analysis. Furthermore, because these issues interact with other disciplines, I felt the need to consider, be it ever so briefly, how the stylistic approach to literary understanding relates to literary criticism, and how stylistic analysis might be applied in support of social reading processes of literary and non-literary discourses in which the reader is ideologically positioned.

Second, the perspective from which I have written this book is also grounded in my personal understanding and interpretation of what I have learnt in the last two decades from two extremely rich sources. One of these has been the fruitful contacts with my professional friends in the Poetics and Linguistics Association (PALA), who have wittingly or unwittingly influenced my thinking about stylistics. The other source of inspiration has been provided by the animated seminar discussions with my students in the Department of English Language and Literature at the University of Amsterdam. In particular, as a result of their responses, I have come to believe very firmly that stylistics can lend strong support to literary critical appreciation by providing textual substantiation for the different kinds of literary effect a text may have on the reader.

I wish to express my warm thanks to Julia Sallabank and Cristina Whitecross at Oxford University Press for their solid support, and in particular for their patience when deadlines had to be extended. A special word of thanks goes to Anne Conybeare. Her scrupulous attention to detail as well as her probing questions regarding content have been of great benefit to this book. Deliberately, I have left the person to whom I owe the greatest debt until last: Henry Widdowson. As a matter of fact, my gratitude to him is far-ranging, because one of his earliest articles was a major influence in converting me to stylistics. Therefore, I was greatly honoured when he generously invited me to write this book. I am also most grateful to him for lavishing on me his outstanding editorial guidance, for reminding me gently now and then of the kind of book he had in mind for (t)his series, and for affording me the full benefit of his vast experience as a writer. I shall miss our regular exchange of friendly messages very much.

PETER VERDONK
Amsterdam, October 2001

Survey

1
The concept of style

Stylistics is concerned with the study of style in language. But what is style in language? How is it produced? How can it be recognized and described? Is it a general feature of language?

The term style (without specific reference to language) is one which we use so commonly in our everyday conversation and writing that it seems unproblematic: it occurs so naturally and frequently that we are inclined to take it for granted without enquiring just what we might mean by it. Thus, we regularly use it with reference to the shape or design of something (for example, 'the elegant style of a house'), and when talking about the way in which something is done or presented (for example, 'I don't like his style of management'). Similarly, when describing someone's manner of writing, speaking, or performing, we may say 'She writes in a vigorous style' or 'She started off in fine style'. We also talk about particular styles of architecture, painting, dress, and furniture when describing the distinctive manner of an artist, a school, or a period. And, finally, when we say that people or places have 'style', we are expressing the opinion that they have fashionable elegance, smartness, or a superior manner (for example, 'They live in grand style' or 'Here one can eat in style').

These everyday notions make a good starting point for a more technical discussion of the use of **style in language**. In one way or another, all of them make reference to a distinctive manner of expression, through whatever medium this expression is given physical shape. Along the same lines, style in language can be defined as distinctive linguistic expression. But, as with other manifestations of style, we need to consider what makes an expression distinctive, why it has been devised, and what effect it has.

So **stylistics**, the study of style, can be defined as the analysis of distinctive expression in language and the description of its purpose and effect. How such analysis and description should be conducted, and how the relationship between them is to be established are matters on which different scholars of stylistics, or stylisticians, disagree, but this general definition will serve our purposes for the present.

To see how this definition works out in practice, let us look at how different **genres**, or types, of text containing specific features of style create particular effects.

Features of style: a newspaper headline

Life on Mars—war of the words

This is a headline from 'The Friday Review' section of *The Independent* of 21 August 1998. It introduces an article reviewing a fierce scientific debate about the possibility of life on Mars. Headline writers use a wide range of devices to create a very specific style, which is sometimes called 'headlinese'. Their one-liners must put in a nutshell the main point of the news story they relate to and at the same time capture the reader's attention. Therefore, an essential feature of headlines is their typographical make-up. They are usually in a larger and bolder typeface than that of the articles they introduce. As a result of the size of the print and the restricted space available in the layout of the page, **ellipsis** (which means that some words have been missed out) is very often a feature of the language of headlines. The result is a succinct, pungent style, which has a direct and powerful effect on the reader. Usually, the omissions can be recovered or guessed from the context. So, if we pad out the above headline, we might get something like 'The life on Mars debate remains a war of words'. It will be noticed that the headline as it stands contains no verb: this is replaced by the dash ($-$). This structure has the effect of all the focus being on the balanced phrases 'Life on Mars' and 'war of the words'.

Though headlines are meant to be read silently, the way their sounds and word-stresses are patterned often appeals to our inner ear. In this headline, for example, the strong stresses on the nouns 'life', 'Mars', 'war', and 'words' are equally divided over the two phrases (hence the balance between them), while the initial sounds of 'war' and 'words' alliterate. Apart from being pleasing to our ears and sense of rhythm, such sound effects add to the attention-drawing aspect and memorability of the headline.

Finally, the phrase 'war of the words' is an excellent illustration of **intertextuality**, i.e. an allusion to another text and, at the same time, an appeal to the reader's awareness of that text. Cultures have produced works of art like novels, poems, plays, and songs, which become familiar to their members. They also generate numerous linguistic expressions like proverbs and sayings, which become equally well-established. It is quite common for writers of all kinds, including headline writers, as we see here, to regularly tap such cultural resources.

In our headline the intertextual allusion is, as it were, heralded by the first phrase 'Life on Mars'. This may kindle the reader's secret fear of Martians invading the world, which in turn accounts for the popular appeal of H. G. Wells's famous science fiction novel *The War of the Worlds*, published in 1898, to which the second phrase 'war of the words' obviously alludes. In fact, for some readers the intertextual echo may be further reinforced if they recollect that in 1938 Orson Welles broadcast a dramatization of the novel in the United States, which stirred up great excitement because millions of listeners mistook it for a factual account of an invasion by Martians. Stylistically, intertextuality appears to have the effect of giving the reader the pleasurable sense of satisfaction at having spotted the allusion, and it may often intensify the overall significance of a text.

Style as motivated choice

Among other things, our investigation of the above headline has confirmed that style is indeed a distinctive way of using language for some purpose and to some effect. It has also demonstrated that in order to achieve his or her purpose and effect, the writer has chosen the fragmentary text 'Life on Mars—war of the words' in preference to a fully-fledged sentence like 'The life on Mars debate remains a war of words'. In fact, all the devices which have been used to create an attention seeking and effective headline are the result of the choice of certain forms and structures over others that could have been chosen but which were not. For instance, the size of the headline's typeface could have been smaller or bigger. In the same way, the words, the patchy grammar, the sound effects, and the pun on another text are all a matter of choice among other possibilities. In identifying what is distinctive and effective, we therefore recognize implicitly what is absent from the text as well as what is actually there in black and white. In short, the choices that have been made can be said to form the headline's stylistic design.

So in making a stylistic analysis we are not so much focused on every form and structure in a text, as on those which stand out in it. Such conspicuous elements hold a promise of stylistic relevance and thereby rouse the reader's interest or emotions. In stylistics this psychological effect is called **foregrounding**, a term which has been borrowed from the visual arts. Such foregrounded elements often include a distinct patterning or parallelism in a text's typography, sounds, word-choices, grammar, or sentence structures. Other potential style markers are repetitions of some linguistic element, and deviations from the rules of language in general or from the style you expect in a particular **text type** or context. (Some instances of these style markers will be discussed later.) What we can conclude from all this is that the concept of style crucially involves choice: it rests on the fundamental assumption that different choices will produce different styles and thereby different effects. If, for instance, the choices of the headline writer had yielded the variant 'Life on Mars is still in dispute', the stylistic impact on the reader would almost certainly have been much less striking.

Style in context

Something else our analysis of the headline has revealed is that style does not arise out of a vacuum but that its production, purpose, and effect are deeply embedded in the particular **context** in which both the writer and the reader of the headline play their distinctive roles. At this point, we should distinguish between two types of context: linguistic and non-linguistic context. Linguistic context refers to the surrounding features of language inside a text, like the typography, sounds, words, phrases, and sentences which are relevant to the interpretation of other such linguistic elements. Most readers will have been able to guess the missing elements in the life-on-Mars headline with the help of the linguistic environment formed by the text of the news story it relates to, and the writer of the headline obviously counted on this linguistic ability.

The non-linguistic context is a much more complex notion since it may include any number of text-external features influencing the language and style of a text. In the case of the life-on-Mars headline, for instance, we may be pretty sure that its writer was, consciously or not, influenced by a wide variety of contextual factors such as the type of newspaper he or she was working for (*The Independent* is a broadsheet British national newspaper); its commercial and editorial policies; its house style; its type of readership; the writer's expectations of the readers' knowledge, anxiety, or scepticism about the possibility of Martian life; the writer's creative talent, attitudes, and beliefs; the writer's expectation that the intertextual allusion will be picked up by the reader, and last but not least, the writer's assumption that newspaper readers have a general knowledge of the social function and stylistic conventions of headlines. If one thing has become obvious from this long, but still incomplete, list of non-linguistic contextual factors, it is the fact that conscious or unconscious choices of expression which create a particular style are always motivated, inspired, or induced by contextual circumstances in which both writers and readers (or speakers and listeners in the case of spoken texts) are in various ways involved.

Style and persuasive effect

The following text is a blurb on the back of Margaret Atwood's collection of short stories *Dancing Girls and Other Stories*:

> This splendid volume of short fiction testifies to Margaret Atwood's startlingly original voice, full of a rare intensity and exceptional intelligence. Each of the fourteen stories shimmers with feelings, each illuminates the unexplored interior landscape of a woman's mind. Here men and women still miscommunicate, still remain separate in different rooms, different houses, or even different worlds. With brilliant flashes of fantasy,

humor, and unexpected violence, the stories reveal the complexities of human relationships and bring to life characters who touch us deeply, evoking terror and laughter, compassion and recognition — and dramatically demonstrate why Margaret Atwood is one of the most important writers in English today.

In the light of our discussion about the strong bond between external context and style, it would be interesting to ask yourself, before reading on, why the style of the above piece, however effective it may be, would not be fitting for a review or an academic essay.

A blurb is a text that publishers print on the jacket or cover of a book to give the potential reader an idea of what it is about, though obviously its primary purpose is to stimulate sales. Our analysis of the newspaper headline, and ensuing development of the notion of style as contextually motivated choice, have shown that writers normally make their style conform to the social function and formal conventions of a particular text type, or genre. They do so because they expect their readers to be socially tuned in to them. Indeed, learning the social functions, conventions, and practices of the endless variety of texts with which we are confronted in the course of our lives is an essential part of our socialization. Accordingly, readers who are familiar with the contextual why and how of blurb writing are likely to read this unconcealed eulogy of Margaret Atwood's writing without any sense of what makes it distinctive. All the same, it remains interesting and instructive to find out what stylistic techniques the writer of this piece has used to 'dramatically demonstrate why Margaret Atwood is one of the most important writers in English today'.

Considering that it is a relatively brief text, what is striking about it is its high proportion of complimentary words and phrases such as 'splendid', 'startlingly original', 'a rare intensity', 'exceptional intelligence', and 'brilliant'. Other words and images are rather emotive, for example, '[Each story] shimmers with feelings', '[each story] illuminates the unexplored interior landscape of a woman's mind', 'unexpected violence', 'the complexities of human relationships', and 'characters who touch us deeply'. Obviously, these loaded vocabulary choices reveal the writer's motive, which is to persuade the reader of the book's excellence.

This persuasive technique is supported by the rhetorical structure of the text as a whole. As a result of there being no sentence linkers like 'therefore', 'because', or 'seeing that', which normally structure an argument, the blurb becomes a mere list of assertive statements without any reasoning. We also find this forceful style inside the sentences, most of which contain lists of two or more exemplifying items linked by commas or the coordinating conjunctions 'and' and 'or', for example: 'full of a rare intensity and exceptional intelligence', 'men and women still miscommunicate, still remain separate in different rooms, different houses, or even different worlds', and 'brilliant flashes of fantasy, humor, and unexpected violence'. Such an additive style can be quite persuasive because the separately listed elements reinforce the assertions the writer makes. Particularly when they are linked by 'and', the separate elements of such lists are even more highlighted as, for instance, in the juxtapositions 'a rare intensity and .exceptional intelligence', 'terror and laughter', and 'compassion and recognition'.

It is mildly ironic that in the conclusion of the blurb the writer seems to admit that it has been 'dramatically' (rather than 'logically') demonstrated that Margaret Atwood is one of the most important writers in English today. Indeed, the persuasion works by dramatic effect rather than rational argument.

Conclusion

We have in this chapter discussed the notion of style in general and how this might be defined with reference to language use in particular. We examined two different texts and identified particular verbal features and the possible effects they might give rise to. We suggested, too, that the effects depend on the reader assuming that these features are a matter of motivated choice on the part of the writer, that they are designed to be noticed. This raises a general question of the relationship between intention and interpretation, which we shall return to in Chapter 3. But meanwhile there is another matter we need to attend to. The texts we have considered so far have been ordinary 'conventional' ones. The second is *about* a work of literature but does not itself have literary pretensions. But what of the style of texts that do claim to be literature?

2

Style in literature

When we encounter a text, we recognize it as of a particular and familiar kind, as belonging to a particular **genre**, for example a newspaper article, a blurb, a menu, or an insurance policy. We have an idea of what to expect, and we adjust our reading accordingly.

Thus, in the course of our discussion about the blurb text in Chapter 1, we concluded that becoming familiar with the functions and stylistic conventions of the numerous **text types,** or genres which we encounter in day-to-day life, is very much part of our socialization in the culture we belong to. Though from an entirely different motivation, as we shall see, in principle this learning process also applies to our getting acquainted with text types which are recognized as literary, such as poems. So if you have become familiar with the stylistic conventions of this genre of texts, you will know that the language of poetry has the following characteristics: its meaning is often ambiguous and elusive; it may flout the conventional rules of grammar; it has a peculiar sound structure; it is spatially arranged in metrical lines and stanzas; it often reveals foregrounded patterns in its sounds, vocabulary, grammar, or syntax, and last but not least, it frequently contains indirect references to other texts.

Text type and style

As we saw in Chapter 1, quite a few of these style features also occur in the texts of the newspaper headline and the publisher's blurb. Indeed, the most important lesson we can learn from our comparative analysis of the styles of these two very different text types is the incontestable fact that there is not always a one-to-one correspondence between text type and style. Perhaps the best illustration of this overlapping of different styles is the language of advertising, though we also find it in political manifestos, slogans, or graffiti.

Text type and function

A possible reason for this quick recognition may be that our socialization, part of which may be described as lessons in social survival, has trained us to immediately perceive the purpose and intended effects, i.e. the social function, of most texts we are confronted with. Clearly, the majority of these texts have some practical function in that they have intentions which can be related to the real world around us. For instance, a headline encourages us to read a news story, a publisher's blurb encourages us to buy a book, and an advertisement is designed to promote a product.

This, of course, prompts the compelling question as to what the function might be of text types or genres like poetry and, by extension, of novels and plays, all of which are traditionally designated as literary texts. This is obviously a difficult question. We may try to formulate an answer by considering the kind of text which is in many ways the most obviously literary—a poem. The first thing we might note is that whatever the function of poetry may be, it bears no relation to our socially established needs and conventions, because unlike non-literary texts, poetry is detached from the ordinary contexts of social life. To put it differently, poetry does not make direct **reference** to the world of phenomena but provides a **representation** of it through its peculiar and unconventional uses of language which invite and motivate, sometimes even provoke, readers to create an imaginary alternative world. Perhaps it is this potential of a literary text which is its essential function, namely that it enables us to satisfy our needs as individuals, to escape, be it ever so briefly, from our humdrum socialized existence, to feel reassured about the disorder and confusion in our minds, and to find a reflection of our conflicting emotions. If this is the case, we might conclude that the function of literature is not socializing but individualizing. With this in mind, let us consider the following poem by Thomas Hardy.

Neutral tones

We stood by a pond that winter day,
And the sun was white, as though chidden of God,
And a few leaves lay on the starving sod;
   —They had fallen from an ash, and were gray.

Your eyes on me were as eyes that rove
Over tedious riddles of years ago;
And some words played between us to and fro
   On which lost the more by our love.

The smile on your mouth was the deadest thing
Alive enough to have strength to die;
And a grin of bitterness swept thereby
   Like an ominous bird a-wing. ...

Since then, keen lessons that love deceives,
And wrings with wrong, have shaped to me
Your face, and the God-curst sun, and a tree,
   And a pond edged with grayish leaves.

Though it is a somewhat simplified statement, we may say that in ordinary communication we use language to make reference to all sorts of items in the material world around us. In this function language is ephemeral, because we tend to forget about it the moment we have identified the items referred to. This use of language for efficient and effective communication is of course common practice. But when language does not refer to our everyday social context, as in literary texts, when it is the only thing available to us to construct an imaginary context, then things are entirely different. Then the language becomes the constant factor to which we have to go back every time we wish to recall what we have imagined.

Unsurprisingly, our awareness and perception of this particular use of language have to be much more astute than in ordinary communication, and we therefore experience the verbal structures of a literary text as elements of a dynamic communicative interaction between writer and reader, in which our expectations are fulfilled or frustrated and our emotions roused or soothed by incentives in the text whenever we turn to it. Of course, given the fact that we all have different expectations and different emotions, the responses to these incentives, and thereby our interpretation of the text as a whole, are bound to differ from reader to reader, and may include total rejection. Here, then, are possible effects we might attribute to some of the verbal patterns in the Hardy poem.

Although the occurrence of personification in language is quite common, for instance, when we attach metaphoric animacy to an inanimate grammatical subject (for example, '*Time* flies'), it seems striking that, with the exception of the first word 'We', all the grammatical subjects in the poem refer to inanimate entities so that they form a foregrounded pattern: '*the sun* was white', '*a few leaves* lay...', '*They [the leaves]* had fallen...and were gray', '*Your eyes on me* were...*eyes* that rove...', '*some words* played...', '*The smile on your mouth*...was...', '*a grin of bitterness* swept...', '*keen lessons*...have shaped...', and '*love* deceives,/and wrings with wrong'.

It is perhaps also somewhat disturbing that, except for her inclusion in the pronoun 'we', the woman (assuming that the speaker in the poem is a man) is consistently reduced to parts of her body: 'your eyes', 'the smile on your mouth', and 'a grin of bitterness'. Now, if we assume that foregrounding produces a psychological effect, this prominent patterning invites the reader's interpretation. In the material world we normally associate human agentive subjects with intention, conscious action or interaction, and control and responsibility. In the textual world of the poem, however, these behavioural notions are undermined by being systematically suppressed. One might therefore be induced to conclude that these two people are inherently powerless to deal with their relationship.

At the same time, one might interpret the completely isolated instance of the only human subject 'we' among all these inanimate ones as representing the utter loneliness of these two people, and their futile struggle against the indifferent, mechanical forces which rule their world, inflicting on them the bitter ironies of their lives and loves.

This reading is supported by a chain of images which call up a sense of utter desolation reflecting the desolate state of their love: a pond on a winter's day, a pale sun as if rebuked by God, a few gray leaves on the dying turf, which have fallen from an ash tree (for me the word 'ash' reinforces the pervasive grayness of the scenery and seems to hint at the extinguished fire of their love), a mirthless smile, a bitter grin, and an ominous bird flying past. Going over these images again, one might notice another fore-grounded pattern, namely that most of them contain a verbal element as if they were the tangible evidence of a series of fateful happenings, for instance, '*chidden* of God', '*starving* sod', '*fallen* from', 'eyes that *rove*', 'a grin of bitterness *swept* thereby', 'the God-*curst* sun', and 'a pond *edged* with grayish leaves'.

When the nature images from the first stanza, and the image of the contorted face of the woman in the middle ones (note the bitter oxymoron 'Alive enough to have strength to die') are emphatically repeated in the final stanza, one realizes that this personal event has been transformed into a symbol for a commonly shared experience. Note that this emphatic repetition also shows in the rhythm of the last two lines in which the main stresses fall heavily on each of the images that the speaker now remembers as bad omens:

Your face, and the God-curst sun, and a tree,
    And a pond edged with grayish leaves.

Furthermore an extra stress is added to the final line, which has four stresses while the final lines of all other stanzas have only three. This is a typical example of **internal foregrounding**, that is, a deviation from a pattern set up by the text of the poem itself.

One might also suggest that this process of transmutation from the particular to the universal is further borne out by the lapse of time between past events and the speaker's present reflection on them, which is expressed by the pattern of verb tenses: the past tense in the first three stanzas and the present perfect 'have shaped to me' in the final one.

Finally, let us complete this brief interpretative engagement with the poem's text with a reflection on its title, 'Neutral Tones'. In addition to the obvious meaning of 'neutral shades of colour', with reference to the neutral tones of white and gray in the scenery described, the phrase may also mean 'indifferent tones of voice', with an obvious allusion to the lovelessness between the two people.

Conclusion

As in Chapter 1, I have identified certain specific features of a text and suggested what effects they might have on the reader. This time, however, the text is a literary one, and I have suggested that there is something distinctive about it which prompts a different kind of response: one which is in a way more individual, more creative. The text seems to alert the reader to some significance which is implied but not made linguistically explicit, which is somehow read *into* the text. The question arises as to whether we can be more precise about these effects, whether we can pin down the differences between literary and non-literary texts that I have suggested. To do this we need to consider more closely the nature of text in general, and this takes us on to the next chapter.

3
Text and discourse

The nature of text

When we think of a **text**, we typically think of a stretch of language complete in itself and of some considerable extent: a business letter, a leaflet, a news report, a recipe, and so on. However, though this view of texts may be commonsensical, there appears to be a problem when we have to define units of language which consist of a single sentence, or even a single word, which are all the same experienced as texts because they fulfil the basic requirement of forming a meaningful whole in their own right. Typical examples of such small-scale texts are public notices like 'KEEP OFF THE GRASS', 'KEEP LEFT', 'KEEP OUT', 'DANGER', 'RAMP AHEAD', 'SLOW', and 'EXIT'.

It is obvious that these minimal texts are meaningful in themselves, and therefore do not need a particular structural patterning with other language units. In other words, they are complete in terms of communicative meaning. So, if the meaningfulness of texts does not depend on their linguistic size, what else does it depend on?

Consider the road sign 'RAMP AHEAD'. When you are driving a car and see this sign, you interpret it as a warning that there will be a small hump on the road ahead of you and that it is therefore wise to slow down when you drive over it. From this it follows that you recognize a piece of language as a text, not because of its length, but because of its location in a particular context. And if you are familiar with the text in that context, you know what the message is intended to be.

But now suppose you see the same road sign in the collection of a souvenir-hunter! Of course, you still know the original meaning of the sign, but because of its dissociation from its ordinary context of traffic control, you are no longer able to act on its original intention. Furthermore, prompted by its alien situational context, you might be tempted to think up some odd meaning for the otherwise familiar sign, particularly when you see it in relation to other 'souvenirs' in the collection. (Needless to say, this is probably exactly what the souvenir-hunter wants you to do.) From this example of alienation of context we can then conclude that, for the expression of its meaning, a text is dependent on its use in an appropriate context.

The nature of discourse

We may go even further and assert that the meaning of a text does not come into being until it is actively employed in a context of use. This process of activation of a text by relating it to a context of use is what we call **discourse**. To put it differently, this contextualization of a text is actually the reader's (and in the case of spoken text, the hearer's) reconstruction of the writer's (or speaker's) intended message, that is, his or her communicative act or discourse. In these terms, the text is the observable product of the writer's or speaker's discourse, which in turn must be seen as the process that has created it. Clearly, the observability of a text is a matter of degree: for example, it may be in some written form, or in the form of a sound recording, or it may be unrecorded speech. But in whatever form it comes, a reader (or hearer) will search the text for cues or signals that may help to reconstruct the writer's (or speaker's) discourse. However, just because he or she is engaged in a process of reconstruction, it is always possible that the reader (or hearer) infers a different discourse from the text than the one the writer (or speaker) had intended. Therefore, one might also say that the inference of discourse meaning is largely a matter of negotiation between writer (speaker) and reader (hearer) in a contextualized social interaction.

So we can suggest that a text can be realized by any piece of language as long as it is found to record a meaningful discourse when it is related to a suitable context of use.

Textual and contextual meaning

At this point, it will have become clear that in order to derive a discourse from a text we have to explore two different sites of meaning: on the one hand, the text's intrinsic linguistic or formal properties (its sounds, typography, vocabulary, grammar, and so on) and on the other hand, the extrinsic contextual factors which are taken to affect its linguistic meaning. These two interacting sites of meaning are the concern of two fields of study: **semantics** is the study of formal meanings as they are encoded in the language of texts, that is, independent of writers (speakers) and readers (hearers) set in a particular context, while **pragmatics** is concerned with the meaning of language in discourse, that is, when it is used in an appropriate context to achieve particular aims. Pragmatic meaning is not, we should note, an alternative to semantic meaning, but complementary to it, because it is inferred from the interplay of semantic meaning with context.

The notion of **context** has already been introduced, if somewhat informally, in the previous chapters. We now need to be more precise. It will be recalled that we distinguished two kinds of context: an internal linguistic context built up by the language patterns inside the text, and an external non-linguistic context drawing us to ideas and experiences in the world outside the text. The latter is a very complex notion because it may include any number of text-external features influencing the interpretation of a discourse. Perhaps we can make the notion more manageable by specifying the following components (obviously, the list is by no means complete):

1 the text type, or genre (for example, an election poster, a recipe, a sermon)
2 its topic, purpose, and function
3 the immediate temporary and physical setting of the text
4 the text's wider social, cultural, and historical setting
5 the identities, knowledge, emotions, abilities, beliefs, and assumptions of the writer (speaker) and reader (hearer)
6 the relationships holding between the writer (speaker) and reader (hearer)
7 the association with other similar or related text types (inter-textuality)

The headline revisited

Let us now try to put these ideas to work by reconsidering our analysis of the newspaper headline 'Life on Mars—war of the words', which we examined in Chapter 1.

When we analysed the headline's stylistic make-up and interpreted its effects, we did so from a double-focused perspective which corresponds to the distinctions just outlined. First we pointed out how the headline writer had exploited the resources of language. To that end we recorded the foregrounded choices which the writer had made from the following elements of the linguistic system: typography (a larger and bolder typeface; the use of a dash in a conspicuous place), sounds and rhythm (alliteration and a balanced stress pattern), grammar and structure (elliptical sentence and two balanced phrases of the same structure), and vocabulary (for example, 'war of words' instead of 'debate', 'dispute', or 'quarrel'). At that stage of our analysis, we were adopting a semantic perspective, that is, we registered these choices as having been made from the linguistic system. In brief, we treated the headline as text.

Next we shifted to a pragmatic perspective by making the point that most of these striking linguistic choices are inevitably motivated by the socio-cultural situation the writer is working in, namely the hectic world of a British national newspaper and its readers. Though only selectively, we indicated some of the contextual factors that are very likely to have influenced the writer's discourse and therewith the text, that is, the medium of his or her discourse. In fact, one might try to tick off the situational features we suggested against the items (1) through (7) on the above list of potential text-external features. Clearly, this move to the world outside the text enabled us to examine the headline's marked linguistic forms in terms of their pragmatic or communicative use, in other words, as a resource to reconstruct the headline writer's discourse. Putting the headline's text into relation with its context also enabled us to express some evaluative judgements about the possible (perhaps intended) effects of the headline writer's foregrounded linguistic choices such as its succinct and pungent style, its direct and powerful effect on the reader and, last but not least, its intertextual allusion. Obviously, these are stylistic and not linguistic judgements, which can only be made, as we have just seen, by relating the linguistic forms of the text to a relevant context of use, that is, by treating it as discourse.

In this connection, the intertextual allusion in the headline is an interesting example of the possibility that some of the newspaper's readers might miss the pun and thereby derive another discourse from the text than the one the writer intended.

The context of literary discourse

But what of literary texts of the kind discussed in Chapter 2? How are these points about text, context, and discourse relevant to them? In principle, the process of discourse inferencing is the same for non-literary and literary texts, for in either case we have to bring about an interaction between the semantic meanings of the linguistic items of the text and the pragmatic meanings these items take on in a context of use. However, as we argued in Chapter 2, the nature of the context of *literary discourse* is quite different from that of non-literary discourse in that it is dissociated from the immediacy of social contact. In very broad terms, whereas the non-literary text makes a connection with the context of our everyday social practice, the literary text does not: it is self-enclosed.

Now, the discourse of daily social life is, of necessity, constantly aimed at the control, categorization, and abstraction of an endless variety of social institutions, relationships, and processes. In fact, the very term 'society' is a prime example of how far we can go in our habitual urge to abstraction! But we also hold dear an altogether different urge, namely the desire to be an individual, to be distinct from others, though realizing at the same time that we are indivisible members of society. It is literature, and in a broad sense all art, which can be said to potentially provide an outlet for these individualizing tendencies. In the case of literature, this escape exists because its discourse is divorced from the context of the social practice we have just described. To put it differently, literary discourse represents a world that refuses to be categorized and pigeon-holed, unlike the social world we live in. It is essential to recognize, however, that the alternative realities represented by literary discourses do not offer a neat and tidy substitute for the realities which we are in the habit of constructing as members of a society. The meanings of *literary* discourses are indefinite, undetermined, unstable, and indeed often unsettling. So every time we try to infer a discourse from the same literary text, we are sure to find other meanings, which again and again will refuse to be pinned down, and may therefore open up a refreshing perspective in addition to our socialized certainties. It is here that Nietzsche's dictum comes to mind 'We have Art in order that we may not perish from Truth'.

All this does not mean, of course, that literary texts bear no relation to the 'real world'. Of course they do, otherwise we would not be able to identify with them and construe some meaningful discourse. The point is that their characteristic use of language, unlike that of non-literary texts, challenges our socializing tendency to align ourselves with abstractions and generalizing concepts. Indeed, literary language brings about this challenge by stressing and, what is even more important, by preserving the particular. Paradoxically, this unique 'verbal pickling' of the particular, to borrow a phrase from Philip Larkin, nevertheless invites or tempts us to look for some broader significance. But, for reasons explained above, we do not socialize this wider meaning, so that it remains inherently individual and thereby always divergent.

The communicative situation in literary discourse

Essentially, I have argued, a discourse is a context-bound act of communication verbalized in a text, and waiting to be inferred from it. Such a communicative act is inherently an interpersonal activity between two parties: the first-person party at the addresser end of the process, and the second-person party at the addressee end. These parties may share a physical context, as in face-to-face conversation, or may not, as in written discourse. But as we have noted, context is not simply a matter of physical circumstances but of the ideas, values, beliefs, and so on inside people's heads. In this sense all communication is a meeting of minds, and meaning is achieved to the extent that the contexts of the two parties come together.

But in literature the communicative situation is not so straightforward. Since, as we have argued, literary texts are disconnected from ordinary social practices, there is a disruption in the direct line of communication between the parties. Thus the first-person pronoun does not represent the person who produced the text but a persona within it, and so we cannot as readers converge on the writer's context but only on that which is internally created in the text itself. And this context may represent not one perspective or point of view, but several.

Let us now illustrate this diversity of perspectives by considering a poem. The author is John Betjeman, and in this respect he is the first-person producer of the text. But whose perspective is represented inside it?

Devonshire Street W.1

The heavy mahogany door with its wrought-iron screen
    Shuts. And the sound is rich, sympathetic, discreet.
The sun still shines on this eighteenth-century scene
    With Edwardian faience adornments—Devonshire Street.

5 No hope. And the X-ray photographs under his arm
    Confirm the message. His wife stands timidly by.
The opposite brick-built house looks lofty and calm
    Its chimneys steady against a mackerel sky.

No hope. And the iron nob of this palisade
10   So cold to the touch, is luckier now than he.
 'Oh merciless, hurrying Londoners! Why was I made
    For the long and the painful deathbed coming to me?'

She puts her fingers in his as, loving and silly,
    At long-past Kensington dances she used to do
15 'It's cheaper to take the tube to Piccadilly
    And then we can catch a nineteen or a twenty-two.'

We might note, first of all, that the scene here is described in third-person terms ('his arm', 'his wife', 'he', 'she') and this presupposes a first-person perspective. The man's plight is related with apparent detachment from the point of view of an uninvolved omniscient narrator, but his or her position is never made explicit by the use of a first-person pronoun: he or she remains an unidentifiable voice. The only times the first-person pronoun makes an appearance are in the **direct speech** of the man (lines 11–12) and of his wife (lines 15–16). But the perspective is different in each case. The wife makes use of the plural 'we' and so speaks on behalf of both of them. The man uses the singular 'I', and although it is *presented* as direct speech, it clearly represents not what he says but what he thinks: it is interior monologue. And of course what the wife says and what he thinks relate to two entirely different realities: the simple and trivial everyday life of the present they can share, and the dreadful agony of the future that they cannot.

So we can discern three perspectives here: that of the man, his wife, and a detached observer. But on closer consideration, things are not so simple. How detached, after all, is the description of the scene here? We might note, for example, that it is heavy with detail. The things described are linguistically realized by rather complex noun phrases, some of which are overloaded with adjectives and other types of modifying elements. In the following list, the head nouns of the noun phrases are in capitals, while the determiners ('the', 'this', 'its'), adjectives (for example 'heavy', 'mahogany'), and other descriptive structures (for example 'with its wrought-iron screen') are in italics:

> *the heavy mahogany* D O O R *with its wrought-iron screen*
> *the eighteenth-century* S C E N E *with Edwardian faience*
>   *adornments—Devonshire Street*
> *the opposite brick-built* H O U S E
> *its* C H I M N E Y S *steady against a mackerel sky*
> *the iron* N O B *of this palisade so cold to the touch*

It should be noted that these complex structures in themselves are just linguistic features, which do not go beyond the status of *textual* data. But, as suggested earlier, we take it that they are designed to have *discourse* significance and so to reflect perspective. The very fact of linguistic elaboration here implies a heightened perception of detail. Who then, we might reasonably ask, would perceive these things in such a way? There would be no motivation for the detached observer to do so, but there would be for somebody who has effectively just received a death sentence. So what we have here, we might infer, is the condemned man's first-person perspective on reality. It would seem that from the moment he leaves the specialist's surgery, his perceiving senses are in a state of high alert: aural ('The heavy mahogany door…

shuts. ...the sound...'), visual ('The sun still shines...adorn-
ments...', 'The...house looks lofty...a mackerel sky'), and tac-
tile ('So cold to the touch').

Of course, we might interpret this detailed awareness in different
ways. Perhaps it intimates the acute sensitivity and heightened
activity of the senses of someone who knows he is going to die,
and therefore now takes in everything around him in a world he
is soon going to leave. Or we may interpret it as suggesting that
the man unconsciously transfers his feelings to these external
objects by contrasting their apparent invulnerability with his
own mortality. Indeed, the solidity and permanence of the things
he perceives are implied by many of their endurable aspects:
the door is made of 'heavy mahogany' and it is provided with
a 'wrought-iron screen'; the scene is 'eighteenth-century' and it
features 'Edwardian faience' (a kind of glazed brick) adornments;
the house opposite is 'brick-built' and looks 'lofty and calm'; its
chimneys look 'steady'; and the nob of the palisade is made
of 'iron'. The doomed patient, we might suggest, seems to be over-
powered by the solidity and agelessness of these lifeless objects,
which ironically emphasize the fragility of his own life and that of
human life in general.

And this assignment of discourse significance might draw our
attention back to the text and to other linguistic features. For
example, there is another conspicuous pattern of linguistic structures in which nouns denoting lifeless objects function either as
the subject of action verbs (the 'door shuts', the 'sun shines', and
the 'X-ray photographs confirm' the message) or as the subject of
copular verbs linked with one or more adjectives denoting human
features (the sound is 'rich, sympathetic, discreet', the 'house looks
lofty and calm', its 'chimneys [look] steady', and the 'nob...is
luckier' than he). Obviously, in itself the clause 'the sun still
shines' is unremarkable, a standard phrase, but it clearly fits and
reinforces this pattern of linguistic structures describing lifeless
things as active and sentient. And it is worth noticing that the
very fact that the expression is normal, even banal, suggests the
continuity of ordinary and accepted things in spite of the man's
personal agony.

In the context of the poem we may construe these structures
pragmatically as a further indication that we are to infer the

man's anxieties and insecurity from the way he perceives the things around him. In fact, it appears that he experiences his surroundings as animated, which implies that lifeless objects are personified. Things are given human attributes in that they are endowed with the power to act by themselves and they are given a consciousness and the human capacity to feel.

By contrast, the ill-fated man is subject of only two verbs. Significantly, both times this is in a context where he is not in control of the situation: in the bitterly ironic comparative clause 'And the iron nob of this palisade...is luckier now *than he [is]*', and in the emotional passive structure 'Why *was I made* for the long and the painful deathbed coming to me?' Obviously, the man thinks he has fallen victim to uncontrollable forces and no longer feels able to perform any action which could change his dreadful situation. In the same way, his wife is made the grammatical subject of helpless actions: 'His wife stands timidly by', and 'She puts her fingers in his as, loving and silly, ...she used to do'.

And again, this inferring of discourse significance might lead us back to the text to see what other textual features might support our interpretation. We might note that there is a consistent use of the simple present tense in the description of the man's perceptions ('the door...*shuts*', 'the sound *is* rich', and 'the X-ray photographs...*confirm* the message'). The use of this tense locates the events in the present, though of course in normal referential terms they cannot be. This gives a perspective of immediacy to the man's experience. His perceptions and his feelings are actual, here and now, not distanced in any past-tense narrative. And the reader of course is drawn into this reality and given a sense of sharing in the immediacy of this contextual present.

Another textual feature which contributes to this effect is the frequent use of the definite article (for example '*the* door', '*the* sound', '*the* X-ray photographs', '*the* message'). The definite article would normally signify a contextual convergence: it specifies something the speaker and the person spoken to both know about. The sick man knows about these things well enough but the reader of course does not, so in normal referential terms the use of the article is not warranted. Its use here, therefore, can be said to confirm that it is the man's perspective on things which is dominant, but also to draw the reader into sharing it.

Conclusion

We have attempted to delineate what might be called a 'communicative triangle', encompassing a first-person party (an addresser), a text as the material manifestation of a discourse, and a second-person party (an addressee). All three are indispensable elements in a dynamic contextualized interaction. It is convenient to talk about text, when our analysis is focused on the intrinsic linguistic properties of the text, without considering its contextual factors. On the other hand, we need the term discourse when our analysis is not only concerned with linguistic features, but also with non-linguistic aspects such as the extra-textual context of communication in which the discourse is situated. In this sense, the term discourse takes text and context together because they are seen as interacting generators of meaning.

Literature is distinctive, I have suggested, because its texts are closed off from normal external contextual connection and this means that we need to infer possible contextual implications, including perspective or point of view, from the textual features themselves. I have illustrated how this works by reference to a poem. But questions of perspective and the variable representation of reality are just as relevant to prose fiction, and that is what we shall turn to in the next chapter.

4

Perspectives on meaning

As we have seen in previous chapters, stylistics is concerned with the possible significance of linguistic features in texts, how they can be interpreted as representing an event or situation from a particular **perspective** or **point of view**. But assigning significance to textual features is far from straightforward, and we must now consider some of the difficulties. To begin with, the notion of perspective is itself problematic.

The double meaning of perspective

One of the regular exhibits in the Rijksmuseum in Amsterdam is a painting by Pieter Saenredam (1597–1665) entitled *Interior of the Church of St Bavo in Haarlem*, 1636. As a result of the perspective the painter has chosen, we look between two pillars into the church, which affords us a clear view of both the main, fifteenth-century organ and a smaller organ. When Saenredam made this painting, music lovers among Haarlem's citizens were petitioning the town council for more organ music in the church. Given this contextual information, it is now thought that Saenredam's motive for depicting the two organs so prominently may have had something to do with this campaign.

This historical anecdote is an apt illustration of the close interconnection between the visual connotations of the word 'perspective' and its mental, emotive, and even ideological orientation. For Saenredam's perspective is not only a point of view in the literal sense, that is a place from which to look at the interior of the church and its two organs. It is also a metaphorical point of view in the sense that, given the historical context, it may be supposed to represent the painter's attitude to, or his sentiments about, organ music in general and the petition of the citizens in particular. There are, after all, other physical viewpoints he might have taken, so why this one in particular? At the same time, this double meaning of perspective also applies to the viewers of the picture. By structuring his painting in this way, Saenredam leads his viewers to imagine that they occupy the very same vantage point as he did, while simultaneously inducing or tempting any perceptive observer to wonder about the deeper significance of the conspicuous positioning (i.e. the foregrounding) of the two organs. So it appears that there is a very close link between literal seeing and metaphorical seeing, between perception and interpretation. Viewers of the picture will readily agree on what visual perspective is presented in the picture. The interpretation of its metaphorical significance is, of course, a much more complex matter.

Perspective in narrative fiction

Though using the different medium of language, writers of narrative fiction exploit this manipulative potential of perspective in a similar way to represent characters, events, and settings of a novel or short story. Clearly, if Saenredam had chosen a different perspective while painting the church interior, he would have produced a different picture, which at the same time would have implied a different attitude to his subject. The same is true of the choice of perspective in a literary fiction: any change in the perspective or point of view from which a fictional world is presented will result in a different story and give rise to a different interpretation.

Or rather to several different interpretations. And here we come up against the most problematic issue in stylistics. As was mentioned in the preceding chapter, we make sense of a text by relating it to the context of our knowledge, emotions, and experience. But since such contexts will be different for particular readers, so interpretations will vary also. The same applies to Saenredam's picture, of course. If you know the historical background, you will be primed to see the perspective as having a local significance as part of the citizens' petition. Otherwise, you might, for example, interpret it as representing the primacy of music in religious worship in general (the organs between the pillars of the church) or simply as an aesthetically pleasing composition with no alternative significance at all. Furthermore, your appreciation of the effect of the perspective, aesthetic or otherwise, will also to some degree depend on your knowledge of the conventions of composition that the artist is presupposing. So when we look at Saenredam's painting, in one sense we all see the same thing, i.e. we can agree that it shows the interior of a church, with pillars, organs, and so on from a particular physical perspective, but we see different things in another sense because we *make sense* of it in different ways.

The same is true of texts. At one level of perception, we might all agree on what a text is about, but diverge greatly in our interpretation of it. And here we have touched on the central issue that stylistics is concerned with: how far can we adduce textual evidence for a particular interpretation, how far can we assign significance to particular textual features? What complicates matters further is that whereas the visual perspective in paintings is easy enough to discern, even if its significance is uncertain, the verbal perspective in texts is not always so easy to identify. This is particularly the case in literary texts, where multiple perspectives come into play. We have already seen this diversity of perspectives in our analysis of the Betjeman poem in the previous chapter, where their identification was shown as relatively unproblematic. But we need now to consider the problem more closely. And we will do so in reference to prose fiction.

The first question that inevitably arises as soon as we start reading a novel or short story is who the narrator is, whose voice we are supposed to be hearing, and therefore whose version of events. We know who the author is, the person who actually produced the text, but that is, of course, not the same thing at all. We have to infer a narrating persona and this we can only do on the internal evidence of the text itself. Consider, for example, the opening of Kazuo Ishiguro's novel *An Artist of the Floating World* (the sentences are numbered for ease of reference):

October, 1948

(1) If on a sunny day you climb the steep path leading up from the little wooden bridge still referred to around here as 'the Bridge of Hesitation', you will not have to walk far before the roof of my house becomes visible between the tops of two gingko

trees. (2) Even if it did not occupy such a commanding position on the hill, the house would still stand out from all others nearby, so that as you come up the path, you may find yourself wondering what sort of wealthy man owns it.

(3) But then I am not, nor have I ever been, a wealthy man. (4) The imposing air of the house will be accounted for, perhaps, if I inform you that it was built by my predecessor, and that he was none other than Akira Sugimura. (5) Of course, you may be new to this city, in which case the name of Akira Sugimura may not be familiar to you. (6) But mention it to anyone who lived here before the war and you will learn that for thirty years or so, Sugimura was unquestionably amongst the city's most respected and influential men.

(7) If I tell you this, and when arriving at the top of the hill you stand and look at the fine cedar gateway, the large area bound by the garden wall, the roof with its elegant tiles and its stylishly carved ridgepole pointing out over the view, you may well wonder how I came to acquire such a property, being as I claim a man of only moderate means.

Here, obviously enough, we have a very distinctive individual voice expressing a subjective perspective which gives an inside view into the mind of a first-person narrator who is also a character in the world of the story. But what kind of character is this? And what kind of mind? Just who the narrator is will emerge later. On his own account so far, he is a person of modest means, even though living in an imposing house. But since this *is* his own account, we cannot, of course, be sure how reliable it is. What can we discover further about what manner of man this is? Since the description of the house figures so prominently in these first paragraphs we might look here for indirect evidence of his character. How then is the house described? It is full of visual detail, almost a picture in words from a spatial perspective:

If on a sunny day you climb the steep path leading up from the little wooden bridge (1);
you will not have to walk far before the roof of my house becomes visible between the tops of two gingko trees (1);
[the house occupies] a commanding position on the hill (2);

the house stand[s] out from all others nearby (2);
as you come up the path (2);
The imposing air of the house (4);
when arriving at the top of the hill you stand and look at the
fine cedar gateway, the large area bound by the garden wall,
the roof with its elegant tiles and its stylishly carved ridgepole
pointing out over the view (7).

Here, we might infer, is somebody with an artist's appreciation of
perspective and spatial composition. However, at certain points in
the narrator's discourse the voice of aesthetic appreciation appears
to intermingle with the voice of materialism, the voice of someone who attaches great importance to property and social status
in spite of his repeated denials. In this light, even some evaluative
expressions in the pictorial descriptions seem to take on a certain
degree of ambivalence: 'a commanding position', 'stand out from
all others' (2) and 'The imposing air of the house' (4). However,
there can be no doubt about the narrator's utterances like 'you
may find yourself wondering what sort of wealthy man owns it'
(2), 'But then I am not, nor have I ever been, a wealthy man' (3), 'he
was none other than Akira Sugimura' (4), 'for thirty years or so,
Sugimura was unquestionably amongst the city's most respected
and influential men' (6), and 'you may well wonder how I came
to acquire such a property, being as I claim a man of only moderate
means'. Note also the repetition of the name of the respected and
influential Akira Sugimura and rhetorical assumptions like 'Of
course, you may be new to this city, in which case the name of Akira
Sugimura may not be familiar to you' (5), and the equally rhetorical assurance 'But mention it to any one who lived here before
the war and you will learn...' (6). Here, we might infer, is somebody deferential to people of power and influence.

So we might say that our first impressions of the unknown
narrator, based on the evidence of this subjective account, are of
an artistic person but one who is, at the same time, influenced by
worldly values.

So far we have been looking at the language of this passage
rather impressionistically to get some sense of who the narrator
is. But we do not normally look at language as outsiders when

reading fiction. The language draws us into the fictional world and we become, in a sense, participants in it. We have already noted how the first-person pronoun signals subjectivity. But there is a corresponding second-person pronoun: the narrator is addressing somebody. Who, then, is it? Somebody, it seems, who might possibly find themselves walking in the locality where the house is and might wonder about its owner. So this would appear to rule out the reader. And yet there is no addressee apparent within the text. And so a kind of second-person vacuum is created, and the reader is drawn in to fill it, and becomes positioned as a participant in the fictional world.

With this in mind, we now turn to consider the text in more detail, and look at how specific linguistic choices can be interpreted as representing the perspective of the first-person narrator and as having the effect of engaging the reader in a second-person role.

Stylistic markers of perspective and positioning

To begin with, at various points in the text the narrator refers to persons, places, and times by means of words and phrases like 'I', 'my', 'you', 'here', 'nearby', and 'this city', and the present and past tenses of verbs, for example 'owns', 'was', 'lived', and 'tell'. In a face-to-face conversation these terms would be easily understood because speaker and listener would share the same physical context of time and place. But in writing, and so in this extract from a novel, things are different. Of course, readers know the textual or semantic meaning of these words, but they do not know their situational or pragmatic meaning. This is because they cannot see the people referred to by 'I', 'my', and 'you' in the flesh, nor can they actually observe the places indicated by 'here', 'nearby', and 'this city', or check the times in relation to the verb tenses. However, prompted by their experience of the real world and their knowledge of the stylistic conventions of fiction, readers will understand these linguistic expressions as **representations** of the people, places, and times in the story, and will act on them as cues to imagine themselves as participating in the situation of the fictional world of the discourse.

Deixis

The technical term for these textual cues is **deictics**, while the psycholinguistic phenomenon as a whole, which is fundamental to all spoken and written discourse, is usually called **deixis** (from a Greek word which means 'pointing' or 'showing'). As we have already seen, deictics may serve to 'point to', or rather direct, the listener's or reader's attention to the speaker's or narrator's spatial and temporal situation. Then there are also deictics which refer the listener or reader to the people taking part in the events of the discourse. Hence we may distinguish three types of deictics: **place deictics** which include adverbs such as 'here' (near the speaker), 'there' (away from the speaker); prepositional phrases like 'in front of', 'behind', 'to the left', and 'to the right; the determiners or pronouns 'this' and 'these' (near the speaker) and 'that' and 'those' (away from the speaker), and the deictic verbs 'come' and 'bring' (in the direction of the speaker) and 'go' and 'take' (in a direction away from the speaker). Another category is **time deictics** which include items such as 'now', 'then', 'today', 'yesterday', 'tomorrow', and 'next Friday'. Other important time deictics are the present and past tenses of full verbs (for example 'play/s', 'played'; 'go/es', and 'went') and of auxiliaries (for example, 'have' and 'had'). The third category is **person deictics**, which include the first person pronoun 'I' (and its related forms 'me', 'my', and 'mine') and the second-person pronoun 'you' (and its related forms 'your' and 'yours'). They are the terms people use to refer to themselves and to talk to each other.

So by persuading readers to assume a presence in the fictional world, the deictics in a narrative text prompt the following important questions: Who is telling the story? Who is the narrator talking to? Where and when do the events take place? And, importantly, from whose perspective is the story told? The deixis in a text may answer this last question, because human beings are cognitively primed to relate the space, time, persons, and objects in the world around them to their own subjective position, that is, to view them from their own point of view. In simpler terms, deixis is speaker-related. A quick look again at the deictics in the Ishiguro text will show that everything in the story world is experienced from the narrator's perspective.

Thus, the place deictics 'here' (1 and 6), 'nearby' (2), 'come' (2), and 'this city' (5) are psychologically lodged in the narrator's spatial self-orientation. This also applies to the time elements expressed by the various present and past verb tenses. As a rule, the present-tense forms of verbs refer to an event-time which can be related to the narrator's *now*, for instance 'owns' (2), 'am' (3), 'inform' (4), and 'tell' (7). The past tense typically refers to an event or situation which is seen as distant from the speaker's *now*. For example, 'was built' (4), 'was' (4 and 6), 'lived' (6), and 'came' (7). These are all pretty straightforward. However, for an interpretation of most of the present tenses related to the narrator's perspective, readers need to remind themselves of the pragmatic ability of speakers to project or extend their presence to some other point in time. For instance, the narrator's *now* has been projected forward to some time in the future in 'If on a sunny day you *climb*' (1), 'before the roof of my house *becomes* visible' (1), 'so that as you *come* up the path' (2), and 'when arriving at the top of the hill you *stand* and *look*' (7). It is clear that, seen from the narrator's perspective, the events represented by the italicized verbs have yet to occur. The choice of the present tense has the effect of bringing them to immediate awareness. Since readers have of course the same cognitive ability as the narrator, the rhetorical effect of this will be that they are prompted to reconstruct this time projection and thus share the narrator's perspective.

Similarly, the person deictics will guide readers to figure out who the 'I' and 'you' are. From their everyday experience, readers know that in ordinary conversation people usually take turns in their roles of speaker and addressee, and as a consequence become sometimes 'I' and sometimes 'you'. Obviously, together with this shift, the point of view changes as well. Significantly, as we have already noted, this turn-taking does not happen in our text because the 'you' does not materialize as an addressee, with the result that the reader is positioned in this role while the perspective remains with the narrator.

What we are seeking to do in this stylistic analysis is to demonstrate how an examination of specific linguistic features of the text can help to substantiate, and perhaps enhance, the impressionistic awareness of its literary effect. And it leads us also to a consideration of other linguistic features which writers use to position readers in the imagined reality of the fictional world.

Given and new information

Consider, for example, how this Ishiguro text exploits the conventional devices for signalling given and new information. **Given information** refers to information which the speaker assumes to be already known to the addressee, because the latter is supposed to have found it in the linguistic or situational context of the discourse, or in the wider context of commonly shared knowledge about the world. So given information provides a kind of background to other elements of the discourse communicating **new information** of which the speaker assumes that the addressee cannot have acquired knowledge from one of the three contextual factors (place, time, person) mentioned above. For instance, in the utterance 'The novel you're thinking of is Tolstoy's *War and Peace*', the definite noun phrase 'The novel you're thinking of' conveys given information because it derives from the context of the preceding discourse, whereas the phrase 'Tolstoy's *War and Peace*' obviously carries new information. Indeed, the definite article 'the' is often an indication of given information, whereas the indefinite article 'a' usually signals new information.

Now in the discourse of Ishiguro's narrator this particular use of the definite article appears to be yet another linguistic device to indicate perspective as well as to engage the reader in the role of addressee. It indicates who controls the perspective because it is the speaker, in this case the narrator, who decides what information must be regarded as given or new. And it has the effect of thrusting the reader, as it were, into the immediate situational context of the narrative because the narrator uses most of the definite articles in the text as if the addressee, and as we have noted by proxy the reader, were actually present on the spot. For instance, the narrator treats the phrases 'the steep path', 'the little wooden bridge' (1), and 'the hill' (2) as given information because he assumes that the addressee can see for him or herself that these objects are there and what they look like. It is as if the narrator points things out to the addressee. This suggestion is particularly strong in the string of definite phrases in sentence (7): 'the fine cedar gateway', 'the large area bound by the garden wall', and 'the roof with its elegant tiles and its stylishly carved ridgepole pointing out over the view'.

While going through the narrative, we might note that the narrator may have other reasons to use the definite article to introduce given information. For example, it might be argued that the narrator uses the definite phrases 'the roof of my house' and 'the tops of two gingko trees' in sentence (1) because the addressee may be assumed to have the general knowledge that houses have roofs and trees have tops. For the same reason, the phrase 'the war' (6) has definite reference because, considering the temporal context (this part of the novel is entitled 'October, 1948') and commonly shared knowledge about the world, the addressee may be supposed to know that the reference is to the Second World War. Obviously, here too, these assumptions on the part of the narrator include and affect the reader.

Ideological perspective

But, of course, the reader cannot be completely included, and so the effect is always ambivalent. As we have seen, the use of certain linguistic devices presupposes reader presence in the context of the story. The narrator talks to the second-person addressee with a marked familiar immediacy, using such emotive expressions as 'you may find yourself *wondering*' (2), 'you will *learn*' (6), and again, 'you may well *wonder*' (7). It is as if he is talking to somebody in his presence who knows who he is. Since no second-person addressee is identified in the text, the reader assumes that position. But of course the reader does not know who he is and so has to somehow construct his identity on the indirect evidence of what he says. Much of this evidence is lexical. Thus, within a relatively brief space, the narrator uses an abundance of evaluative words and phrases like 'commanding' (2), 'wealthy' (2) and (3), 'imposing' (4), 'none other than' (4), 'most respected and influential' (6), 'fine' (7), 'elegant' (7), 'stylishly carved' (7), and 'only moderate' (7). These words are clearly attitudinal, in that they originate from the narrator's **ideological perspective** and convey the subjective nature of his perceptions and observations. And these, as we have noted earlier, seem to hint at an inner conflict of ideologies, an ambivalence of attitude.

And this ambivalence seems to be reflected too in the narrator's use of another linguistic device for signalling attitude, namely modality. **Modality** provides speakers with the linguistic means to express degrees of commitment to the truth or validity of what they are talking *about*, and to mitigate the effect of their words on the people they are talking *to*. In other words, it is used to position the first person both in relation to what they are saying and who they are addressing. And when we look at how modality is used in the Ishiguro text, we notice that the narrator uses one or two modal auxiliaries in nearly every sentence: 'will' in (1), (4), and (6) expresses assumption or certainty; 'would' in (2) certainty; 'may' in (2) and (5) possibility, while 'may not', also in (5), expresses negative possibility, and finally 'may well' in (7) conveys a strong possibility. Our narrator also uses some **sentence adverbs**, which express the modality of the whole sentence or clause, in that they convey his attitude towards what he is claiming: 'The imposing air of the house will be accounted for, *perhaps*' (4), and 'Sugimura was *unquestionably* amongst the city's most respected and influential men' (6).

So there are many indicators of attitudinal position in evidence here. But again the evidence suggests ambivalence: sometimes the narrator seems to be confidently assertive, sometimes tentative. It is difficult to pin his position down. And this seems to be borne out by the very syntax he uses. His sentences are formal and carefully wrought: they unfold as complete and finished patterns without a flaw. Their very measured correctness can be said to reflect an ordered and analytic mind, and one disposed to propriety and decorum. At the same time, the style seems just a touch *too* well organized, so controlled as to seem contrived, and we might suspect that the surface features of the narrator's syntax, suggestive as it is of coherence and logical control, is being used to disguise an underlying conflict of attitude. As was mentioned earlier, an impressionistic reading of the text suggests a certain ambivalence on the part of the narrator about materialistic and aesthetic values, and again we can see how a closer scrutiny of the language can lend support to impressions of this kind.

Conclusion

In this chapter I have tried to show that reading a novel is not only a matter of finding out *what* is told, but also *how* it is told. In other words, you cannot separate content (the 'what') from form (the 'how'). Undoubtedly, the most important formal aspect is the author's choice of perspective. It is the controlling consciousness through whose filter readers experience the events of the story. Thus, we have seen how a subjective first-person perspective can draw readers into the illusion of presence in the fictional world by inducing them to fill the vacant role of the second-person addressee, and how this raises issues about the identity and attitudinal positioning of the first-person narrator. What I have tried to show is how these literary effects can be related to linguistic features of the text, and how such a stylistic analysis might contribute to a clarification, and further exploration, of the readers' impressionistic understanding of a literary work.

In Chapter 5, we shall look at other narrative perspectives as well as at other kinds of literary effect and the linguistic features that can be adduced to account for them.

5

The language of literary representation

In Chapter 4 we examined how the fictional world is represented with reference to the notion of perspective, looking in particular at how language is used to express the subjective perspective of a first-person narrator and how this affects the positioning of the reader. But, of course, language is used in literature to achieve other modes of representation, and these will be our concern in this present chapter. We begin by considering narrative perspectives other than that of the first person.

Perspective in third-person narration

The first-person narrator, as we have seen, necessarily assumes a participant role within the fictional context and so adopts a subjective perspective on events. We might propose that the third-person narrator, on the other hand, takes up the non-participant role of observer and so adopts an objective point of view. But things are not so simple. In the non-fictional world, it is true, the normal convention would be to use third-person terms of reference to talk about objective events that can be observed and reported on: 'The woman was sitting at her table writing letters. She was wearing a red dress. The man entered the room. He picked up a book.' And so on. This is straightforward enough. But in fiction we frequently find that the narrator uses third-person reference to describe things which it is quite impossible to observe. Consider, for example, the following passage from Chapter 8 of D. H. Lawrence's novel *Women in Love* (again, the sentences are numbered for ease of reference):

(1) He went into her boudoir, a remote and very cushiony place. (2) She was sitting at her table writing letters. (3) She lifted her face abstractedly when he entered, watched him go to the sofa, and sit down. (4) Then she looked down at her paper again.

(5) He took up a large volume which he had been reading before, and became minutely attentive to his author. (6) His back was towards Hermione. (7) She could not go on with her writing. (8) Her whole mind was a chaos, darkness breaking in upon it, and herself struggling to gain control with her will, as a swimmer struggles with the swirling water. (9) But in spite of her efforts she was borne down, darkness seemed to break over her, she felt as if her heart was bursting. (10) The terrible tension grew stronger and stronger, it was most fearful agony, like being walled up.

The first six sentences here report observable events from a third-person perspective in a conventional way: 'He went…She was sitting…writing letters. She lifted her face…he entered, watched him…she looked down…He took up a large volume…His back was…'. But with (7) there is a transition to a different perspective. If this sentence had read 'She stopped writing', or 'She did not go on with her writing', then the passage would continue in the same third-person vein as before. But 'She could not go on with her writing' expresses a state of mind which is inaccessible to observation, and which only she herself can be aware of. Sentences (8) to (10) then follow suit and directly express the personal experience of the character. The narrator has moved, so to speak, inside the character's mind. And so we have a convergence of what would conventionally be distinct perspectives: a third-person expression of first-person experience. And as the perspective changes, so does the use of language. The most obvious difference is in sentence length. The text on each side of the transitional sentence (7) consists of exactly the same number of words (68) but they combine into six sentences in the first part and only three in the second. But the sentences do not only differ in length, but also in their syntax. Those of the first part of the text are structurally straightforward and describe a sequence of events in an orderly linear way: 'He went…she was sitting…She lifted her face…he entered

…[she] watched him…' and so on. After the transition, however, the syntax becomes disordered, phrases do not fit together with neat linearity, but accumulate without clear structural connections. What is expressed is not a series of events but a sudden outbreak of sensations all happening at the same time. The chaos in Hermione's mind, and her struggle for the control of her feelings, are, we might say, not just described, but directly represented by the syntax itself.

In this text, then, we see a shift in narrative perspective from that of the third-person observer to that of first-person participant, and a corresponding change in the way language is structured to achieve an appropriate representation. The narrator is not bound by the normal conventions of third-person reference, but is in effect a kind of omniscient witness. At one time the narrator might describe things from a detached perspective distinct from that of the characters. This is the case in the first part of the text where, we might note in passing, it is underscored by asides like 'a remote and very cushiony place' (hardly the way Hermione would describe her boudoir), and the ironic comment '[he] became minutely attentive to his author'. So at one time, then, the narrator may be the outsider looking on. But at another time we find a quite different perspective: that of the insider who can reveal the most intimate and innermost experiences of the characters themselves.

In the Lawrence text, the narrator shifts perspective but remains within one fictional context of time and place. But narrators can also shift perspective by taking up different contextual positions. They can be not only omniscient but also omnipresent. A particularly striking example of this is Thackeray's description of George Osborne's death at the Battle of Waterloo in Chapter 32 of his novel *Vanity Fair*:

> No more firing was heard at Brussels—the pursuit rolled miles away. Darkness came down on the field and city; and Amelia was praying for George, who was lying on his face, dead, with a bullet through his heart.

The omnipresent narrator can be in different contexts at the same time ('at Brussels', 'miles away','on the field and city'), and, as he is also omniscient, he knows what is going on there ('No more firing...', 'the pursuit...', 'Darkness...'), and has exact information about the contemporaneous situations of the different characters ('and Amelia was praying for George, who was lying on his face...').

Again, what is of interest here is how language is used to represent this unique multiple perspective on events and to draw the reader into sharing it. We might note, to begin with, that two kinds of verbal structure occur in the description: the simple past ('was heard', 'rolled', 'came down') and the past progressive ('was praying', 'was lying'). Since the first of these conventionally expresses completed action at a point in time, it is appropriate for it to be used here in clauses which set the scene and locate events in time and place. These verbs serve as a general contextual background, we might say, against which the more particular events relating to the individual characters are to figure. And these are described in the past progressive, again appropriately, since we are thereby induced to dwell upon them. So we might conclude that the events described in the past simple clauses serve as **ground**, with what is described in the past progressive clauses made more prominent as the **figure**.

But there is something about our text that does not quite fit this conclusion. The text consists of two orthographic sentences and we might expect to find all of the simple past ground clauses to be in the first, and the past continuous figure clauses in the second. Instead, we find that the third of the ground clauses ('darkness came down...') has encroached into the second sentence. It would seem to be more satisfactory for the text to have the form: (Ground) 'No more firing was heard in Brussels—the pursuit rolled miles away, and darkness came down on the field and city. (Figure) 'Amelia was praying for George...'. But that is not what Thackeray wrote. So how do we account for his version of events?

Let us look again at these clauses. Notice that although the fourth of them ('Amelia was praying for George') is different in verb form from the first three, it is like them in that it is a main clause. As such it completes a pattern of four clauses which are similar in structural simplicity, length, and rhythm:

No more firing was heard in Brussels—the pursuit rolled miles away.

Darkness came down on field and city, and Amelia was praying for George, ...

The similarity of these four structures seems to suggest that they are all functioning alike to list a series of happenings, so that Amelia praying for George is represented as an event of the same kind as the pursuit rolling away and the darkness falling. And the list seems to be complete: the 'and' that precedes the final clause seems to signal that it is the last of a sequence and rounds off the pattern, and it is a complete clause as it stands, and syntactically needs no further extension.

But extended it is, by the continuative relative clause 'who was lying on his face'. And since the earlier delineated patterning carries the implication of closure, the extension comes as a surprise. We are quite unprepared for George's death. We do not expect such momentous news to appear in a subordinate clause, almost as if it were added on as an afterthought. But from one perspective, of course, that of the large-scale events of the battle, it is not momentous, but a relatively minor event, given appropriately incidental mention in a dependent relative clause. From Amelia's perspective, on the other hand, it *is* momentous, and her perspective, we might say, is represented by the use of the past progressive which links the two distanced events of her praying and George's lying dead. And of course the shock the reader feels at the abrupt announcement of his death is a representation too of what she will feel when she gets the news. It is perhaps worth noting that this moment is not actually described in the novel. It does not need to be: the use of language in this text has already given the reader the experience on Amelia's behalf.

Speech and thought representation

We have been looking at examples of a type of third-person omniscient narrator from whose shifting point of view the reader perceives event and character. There are also times, however, when the narrator delegates perspective to the characters and leaves them to speak for themselves. In this case we are presented with a record of **direct speech** (**DS**). We have already encountered an example of this in the poem by John Betjeman in Chapter 3. The last verse runs as follows:

> She puts her fingers in his as, loving and silly,
>> At long-past Kensington dances she used to do
> 'It's cheaper to take the tube to Piccadilly
>> And then we can catch a nineteen or a twenty-two.'

In the first two lines the narrator first describes what happens in the observable present ('She puts her fingers in his') and then shifts to an omniscient perspective to express her feelings, and to recall her personal past. In the last two lines we are presented with the direct speech of her actual utterance.

In the preceding verse of the poem, we also find lines within quotation marks, but here they do not express what the character actually says but what is going on in his mind.

> No hope. And the iron nob of this palisade
>> So cold to the touch, is luckier now than he.
> 'Oh merciless, hurrying Londoners! Why was I made
>> For the long and the painful deathbed coming to me?'

What is presented here is **direct thought** (**DT**), which, unlike DS, does of course, presuppose a privileged omniscience on the part of the narrator. We should note, however, that even when we get DS, the narrator, though temporarily absent, is still there pulling the strings. It is he, or she, after all who decides when it is contextually appropriate for the characters to be left to speak for themselves. Sometimes, indeed, the very absence of narratorial intervention seems to have significant effects. The work of Ernest Hemingway is a case in point. Typically it adopts the mode of objective reporting and the direct presentation of utterances. Here is an example from his short story 'Hills Like White Elephants':

> 'The beer's nice and cool,' the man said.
> 'It's lovely,' the girl said.
> 'It's really an awfully simple operation, Jig,' the man said. 'It's not really an operation at all.'

The girl looked at the ground the table legs rested on.

'I know you wouldn't mind it, Jig. It's really not anything. It's just to let the air in.'

The girl did not say anything.

'I'll go with you and stay with you all the time. They just let the air in and then it's all perfectly natural.'

Here there is hardly any narrator mediation. In the first three utterances reporting clauses are used minimally to indicate who the speakers are ('the girl said', 'the man said') but we get no information about the manner in which the characters said the things they said ('"No," she said absently' or 'he murmured encouragingly'). What little description of the context we get is strictly objective and observable: we are told that the girl 'looked at the ground', but not what she was thinking. One effect of this is to provoke the reader into inferring what this 'it' is that the man is talking about (presumably an abortion), what the girl's thoughts and feelings might be, what their relationship is, and so on. The very baldness of the description and directness of the dialogue thus creates a kind of vacuum which the reader is drawn in to fill.

But the use of DS is not the only kind of speech representation we find in fiction. **Indirect speech** (**IS**) is also common, as indeed it is in non-literary use. Thus the first utterance in the Hemingway passage could be rendered as follows:

The man said (that) the beer was nice and cool.

In the case of IS, the narrator reports only the content of what the character has said, but not its exact wording (it is, in this sense, *reported* rather than *recorded* speech). This allows the narrator to intervene and to interpret the character's original words, thereby, again, shifting perspective:

The man commented on how nice and cool the beer was.

The man said, appreciatively, that the beer was nice and cool.

The representation of **indirect thought** (**IT**), of course, presupposes an even greater degree of narrator initiative:

The man thought that the beer was nice and cool.

These ways of representing direct and indirect speech and thought conform to linguistic conventions which apply to written language in general. We move on now to a kind of representation which is more specifically literary. Consider the following:

The man drank the beer. Goodness, how nice and cool it was!

The expression 'Goodness', suggests a direct record of what was said or thought ('Goodness, how nice and cool it is') but the past tense 'was' suggests that this is an indirect report ('He said/thought how nice and cool it was'). What we have here is a blend of both, a hybrid form. This has been referred to as **free indirect speech** (**FIS**) or **free indirect thought** (**FIT**). At this point, it should be noted that it has become customary to roll the FIS and FIT forms into one and to use the umbrella term **free indirect discourse** (**FID**), and as it appears convenient, we shall adopt this practice in the following discussion of the two free indirect versions of speech and thought presentation.

As with the third-person pronouns in the passage from *Women in Love*, FID brings into convergence the perspectives which would conventionally be kept distinct: that of the narrator looking on and that of the inner experience of the character. So on the one hand we can sense the presence of an intruding narrator who mediates between character and reader, whereas on the other hand we can also detect vestiges of the character's original speech or thought. Obviously, this double-edged reading experience may cause ambiguity as to whose voice we are hearing. In other words, can we attribute what we read to the narrator, or to the character, or to both? This ambiguity may occur particularly when sentences or clauses with FID features are interspersed with what looks like straightforward third-person narrative. This gives FID a rich potential for literary effects such as irony. It is not surprising, therefore, that since the time of Jane Austen (who actually developed it) this technique has become particularly prominent in modern fiction.

Let us now see how FID works in a passage from D. H. Lawrence's short story 'The Shadow in the Rose Garden', in which the unrelenting alternation of the viewpoints of 'he' and 'she' (they are husband and wife) acts out, as it were, the bitterness and resentment of an ill-fated marriage:

(1) He opened the door.

(2) 'Dinner is on the table,' he said.

(3) It was difficult for her to endure his presence, for he would interfere with her. (4) She could not recover her life. (5) She rose stiffly and went down. (6) She could neither eat nor talk during the meal. (7) She sat absent, torn, without any being of her own. (8) He tried to go on as if nothing were the matter. (9) But at last he became silent with fury. (10) As soon as it was possible, she went upstairs again, and locked the bedroom door. (11) She must be alone.

The first sentence is clearly straightforward narrative, while (2) is in direct speech. It is striking that we only get this banal piece of information in the direct form. May we conclude from this that, for the rest, the narrator finds the marital problems of this couple too complex for a more direct style of narration?

In the first clause of (3), 'It was difficult for her to endure his presence', we are confronted with a possible ambiguity. It might be a narratorial statement about the wife's feelings. This would assume that the narrator uses his omniscience to tell us that he knows that it was difficult for her to bear her husband's presence. It would furthermore assume that the wife was not consciously aware that she could not stand being in his company. Then, in the second clause, 'he would interfere with her', you will notice the modal auxiliary 'would'. Usually, such an auxiliary is a marker of character consciousness in FID because it expresses a personal attitude towards a particular situation or event, which an objective third-person narrator is normally not supposed to adopt. In this context 'would' appears to convey that the wife finds it typical of her husband to meddle in her affairs and that she is irritated by such behaviour. Significantly, the two clauses of (3) are linked by the conjunction 'for'. Since this indicates the reason why the statement 'It was difficult for her to endure his presence', was made in the first clause, it might be that, after all, it may be taken to reflect the wife's emotional state and therewith her perspective.

Importantly, the clause 'It was difficult for her to endure his presence' in (3) illustrates that a narrator may also display a character's inner perspective by describing her sentiments without recording her thoughts in the strict sense of the word. In the final instance, however, the ambiguity remains unsolved. This is also because in longer stretches of discourse, FID is not purely a matter of formal features which can be easily ticked off. Often whether we take it as indicating the intrusion of the narrator or the consciousness of the character must also be based on contextual evidence in the discourse, which may even include the plot of the story or novel as a whole.

Then (4) features the modal 'could' as a sign of FID, and we can read this as the narrator inducing the reader to share the character's point of view. However (5) may be safely looked upon as a piece of straightforward narrative.

Our stylistic purpose, here and elsewhere, is to relate literary effect to specific linguistic features of the text, and as with our previous analyses, we need to consider what other features can be adduced to complement our interpretation. And again we return to pronouns. In this text, the characters are minimally identified by the pronouns 'he' and 'she'. There is no proper name, no descriptive phrase, nothing but the bare prenominal indication of sex, and this is, in fact, not only a feature of this passage but of the whole story.

What are we to make of this? Such pronoun use suggests, perhaps, a diminution of identity, whereby the characters are reduced to their elemental and conflicting sexual differences, with the individual personalities that they *could* engage with closed off inside themselves. Such estrangement is consistent with the use of FID, which, as we have seen, combines third-person distancing with an expression of first-person experience. The last sentence of the passage (11) is a particularly striking example of this, 'She must be alone' being the FID version of 'I must be alone'.

A further development of these modes of thought representation is to be found in the so-called **stream of consciousness technique** through which the narrator designs a style which creates the illusion that, without his or her interference, readers have direct access to the mental processes of the characters, i.e. to their inner points of view. As a result, the reader sees the fictional world through the 'mental window' of the observing consciousnesses of the characters. Because readers receive little if any guidance from the narrator, they have to form their own judgements not only of how the characters experience their fictional universe but also of the value systems which the latter use for assessing it.

Stream of consciousness is now widely used in modern fiction as a narrative method to reveal the character's unspoken thoughts and feelings without having recourse to dialogue or description. Here is an example from Episode 13 (Nausicaa) of James Joyce's *Ulysses*:

Ba. What is that flying about? Swallow? Bat probably. Thinks I'm a tree, so blind. Have birds no smell? Metempsychosis. They believed you could be changed into a tree from grief. Weeping willow. Ba. There he goes. Funny little beggar. Wonder where he lives. Belfry up there. Very likely. Hanging by his heels in the odour of sanctity. Bell scared him out, I suppose. Mass seems to be over. Could hear them all at it. Pray for us. And pray for us. And pray for us. Good idea the repetition. Same thing with ads. Buy from us. And buy from us.

This piece of first-person discourse takes us right into the mind of Mr Leopold Bloom, the central figure in the novel. His thought processes are directly projected. There is no sign here of FID: we do not get 'What was that flying about?' but 'What is that flying about?' The fragmented syntax, the staccato phrases, the use of the present tense, all create a style which dramatizes, as it were, the unedited thoughts and impressions of the character as they occur. The experience is expressed in all its immediacy. And all orientational expressions like 'There he goes' and 'Belfry up there' are related to Bloom's point of view; he is the centre of everything that is going on. And, equally important, the narrator has covered all his tracks in the sense that the extract is entirely free from reporting clauses and quotation marks.

In sum, this is the style of the **interior monologue**, through which the reader is enabled to tune in to the character's train of thought or stream of consciousness, seemingly without being hampered by the presence of the narrator: seemingly, because in reality of course everything is stage-managed by the narrator. It is his or her artfulness, in both senses of the word, that creates the illusion.

We might compare this passage from Joyce with the following from Virginia Woolf. These are the opening lines of her novel *Mrs Dalloway*:

(1) Mrs Dalloway said she would buy the flowers herself.
(2) For Lucy had her work cut out for her. (3) The doors would be taken off their hinges; Rumpelmayer's men were

coming. (4) And then, thought Clarissa Dalloway, what a morning—fresh as if issued to children on a beach.

(5) What a lark! (6) What a plunge! (7) For so it had always seemed to her when, with a little squeak of the hinges, which she could hear now, she had burst open the French windows and plunged at Bourton into the open air. (8) How fresh, how calm, stiller than this of course, the air was in the early morning; like the flap of a wave; the kiss of a wave; chill and sharp and yet (for a girl of eighteen as she then was) solemn, feeling as she did, standing there at the open window, that something awful was about to happen; looking at the flowers, at the trees with the smoke winding off them and the rooks rising, falling; standing and looking until...

The stream of consciousness representation is different here. This is not an interior monologue, if only because it is narrated in the past tense as well as in the third person, and these features create a distancing perspective. Besides, we can spot the narrator's presence not only in the reporting clause 'Mrs Dalloway said' in the very first sentence, but also in the presentation of thought in the clause 'thought Clarissa Dalloway' in (4). So Woolf's style is very much unlike Joyce's stream of consciousness or interior monologue, which, as we have seen, is marked by a 'narrator-free' recording of a character's flow of thoughts in the first person and simple present tense.

Going back to the passage from *Mrs Dalloway*, you will also have observed that apart from (1) and (4), quoted above, all the other sentences in this extract are in FID. As we have seen in the passages by Hemingway and Lawrence, this mix of narrative styles may produce a double-edged effect: on the one hand, the narrator may create a distancing from the character, while on the other hand, he or she may give the reader a sense of nearness to the character's consciousness. For instance, the three brief clauses 'For Lucy had her work cut out for her', 'The doors would be taken off their hinges', and 'Rumpelmayer's men were coming', are apparently representations of Mrs Dalloway's mental checklist of all the things to be done. Furthermore, contextual factors such as the non-introduced names of 'Lucy' and 'Rumpelmayer' clearly belong to Mrs Dalloway's world and therefore suggest that we are in her consciousness. Also, in the exclamations in (5) and (6) we apparently hear the character's inner voice.

In particular, (8) illustrates another important aspect of Virginia Woolf's handling of the stream of consciousness technique, namely that it allows the FID narrator to shape a particular version of the character's consciousness in terms of images or metaphors, which need not be the actual words or thoughts as the character expressed them.

Conclusion

In this chapter we have sought to demonstrate procedures of stylistic analysis whereby specific linguistic features are identified and adduced to support literary interpretation. For the purpose of this demonstration we have focused attention on how perspective is achieved through different modes of speech and thought representation, and how these are complemented by other linguistic features of the text. There are other textual features, of course, which we might subject to close scrutiny as well. We could examine, for example, how language is patterned, particularly in poetry, by the intricate interplay of metrical, lexical, and grammatical features to give distinctive shape to experience. We will be touching on this, and other aspects of literary language in Chapter 6. We will also consider how the stylistic approach to literary understanding that we have been exemplifying relates to other ways of looking at literature.

6
Perspectives on literary interpretation

One of the main themes in previous chapters has been how different perspectives or points of view in literary texts can be inferred from a close analysis of their linguistic features. Such a stylistic approach itself, of course, exemplifies a perspective, namely a perspective on the study of literature, and although this is the one that is explored in this book, it should be emphasized that it is not the only one, nor is it distinct from all others. In this chapter, we will consider other ways of looking at literature, and how stylistics can complement them.

There is another matter we shall also need to consider. With one or two exceptions in previous chapters, we have so far been applying stylistic analysis to literary texts, but the question naturally arises as to why it should not be applied to non-literary texts in like manner, and this is a question we shall take up in the next, and final, chapter of this book. For the moment, however, we continue to focus attention on literature.

Literary criticism

The scholarly study of literature, long established under the name of literary criticism, has yielded a vast amount of insightful commentary, both on individual works and on the sociocultural and aesthetic trends that they exemplify. Whereas, generally speaking, literary criticism directs attention to the larger-scale significance of what is represented in verbal art, stylistics focuses on how this significance can be related to specific features of language, to the linguistic **texture** of the literary text. Thus, early in Chapter 5, we picked on a particular extract from Thackeray's

Vanity Fair to illustrate how language was used to dramatic effect to describe the death of George Osborne at the Battle of Waterloo. Literary critics would be concerned with locating this event in the structure of the whole narrative, with the interplay of character, the relationship between plot and theme, and so on. Or they might look at the extent to which this novel keys in with others by the same author as expressive of his particular artistic vision, or is typical of the period in its genre or ideological position. The fine-grained analysis of texture cannot of itself reveal these features of the fictional work. What it can do is to provide supporting evidence for interpretation by indicating how the macro features that the literary critic is concerned with might be reflected in the micro features of linguistic texture. So we can recognize an interdependency of the perspectives of stylistics and literary criticism, which was exemplified in our discussion of Ishiguro's novel *The Artist of the Floating World* in Chapter 4, where observations about the linguistic particulars of the narrator's description of his house were related to the theme of the novel as a whole.

The same point might be made about poetry. But there is a difference. When dealing with prose fiction, detailed stylistic analysis of the kind we have been illustrating is too time-consuming to be applied to the whole text of a novel but can only be applied to extracts, and the selection of such extracts already presupposes the kind of significance that a literary critical perspective would reveal. It should be pointed out in passing, however, that this is not to say that the whole text cannot be linguistically analysed, and indeed, with the advent of the computer, it is a relatively straightforward process to reveal profiles of textual patterning on a vast scale. Such profiles are of considerable interest in identifying the lexical and grammatical properties which characterize the style of a particular author or period. In this sense, such analysis can be called stylistic, but although it may often prompt further critical enquiry, it is only when such an enquiry is pursued and the significance of these linguistic features explored that we undertake stylistic analysis in the way it has been described in this book.

Such analysis, then, is, in prose fiction, applied not to whole texts but to extracts. Poems, however, are often short, and in this case analysis can range over the entire text, as we saw in

Chapter 3 in the discussion of the poem by John Betjeman. Again, we can see that the stylistic and literary critical perspectives are complementary.

Interpreting a complete poem

To give further illustration of this, let us consider a poem by Seamus Heaney. It is the fourth from a sequence of eight sonnets entitled '"Clearances": *In memoriam M.K.H., 1911–1984*':

> Fear of affectation made her affect
> Inadequacy whenever it came to
> Pronouncing words 'beyond her'. *Bertold Brek*.
> She'd manage something hampered and askew
> 5 Every time, as if she might betray
> The hampered and inadequate by too
> Well-adjusted a vocabulary.
> With more challenge than pride, she'd tell me, 'You
> Know all them things.' So I governed my tongue
> 10 In front of her, a genuinely well-
> Adjusted adequate betrayal
> Of what I knew better. I'd *naw* and *aye*
> And decently relapse into the wrong
> Grammar which kept us allied and at bay.

What are we to make of this poem? At the most obvious level it is about the relationship between a first-person 'I' and a third-person 'she'. We might suppose that the 'I' is the poet himself, but who is the 'she'? The title of the sequence provides the clue: it is written in memory of 'M.K.H.' As is often the case, the title of the poem serves as a point of reference to the external world. The initials M.K.H refer to the poet's mother, Margaret Kathleen Heaney.

On a first reading of the poem we might say that it is about the intellectual and emotional rift which has grown between mother and son as a result of his superior education, and the consequent conflict between maternal and filial love. We might then use the poem as a way into literary biography, and discuss the poet's life and family background. But although the poem can be used as a point of reference in this way, what is distinctive about it as literature is that the conflict it deals with is not described in referential terms but is represented as experience, and it is this which creates the literary effect we react to as readers. Thus we might talk about the impression we get of a certain ambivalence of attitude on the part of the poet: the mother and son adapt considerately to each other, but this is at the same time expressed as a kind of betrayal. The impression we get is of affection competing with exasperation, a struggle with contradiction. This sense of struggle seems to have something to do with the repetition of certain words and their derivatives ('adequate', 'hampered', 'adjust', and 'betray'). Such repetition seems to suggest too a certain awkwardness, as if the poet did not quite know how to express his feelings, and this seems to be consistent with the irregularity of the metre and the clumsiness of the rhyme. As one literary critic, Ian Hamilton, put it, the poem is 'almost breathtakingly ill-made' (*The London Review of Books*, 1 October 1987). This is all the more striking when one realizes that all this rough-hewn language is nevertheless put into the formal poetic design of the sonnet.

So much for the general impression of the literary effect of this poem. The question for stylistics is how far a closer analysis of the linguistic texture of the poem can substantiate and extend this impression.

Substantiation by analysis

Let us begin with the first three lines of the poem:

> Fear of affectation made her affect
> Inadequacy whenever it came to
> Pronouncing words 'beyond her'. *Bertold Brek.*

If we assume that the structure of language consists of the four levels set out below, these three lines provide an interesting example of how specific artistic choices at these levels interact and thus create particular textual patterns which provoke the reader to cull from them some representational effect:

graphology	↔	typographical features
phonology	↔	rhyme, metre, assonance, alliteration
lexis	↔	vocabulary, metaphor, and other figures of speech
syntax	↔	grammatical structures

For instance, on the level of lexis the emotive power of the Germanic word 'fear', right at the beginning of the poem, appears to be offset by the cool and dispassionate effect of the following string of Latinate words: 'affectation', 'affect', 'inadequacy'. Are we led to think that the mother's fear of showing off must not be taken too seriously? At the same time, these Latinate words seem somewhat pretentious in this context and therefore effectively reinforce the mother's ironic game of pretence. Note that on the phonological level this lexical effect is borne out by the pattern of labiodental fricatives ('*Fear*', 'a*ffect*ation', 'a*ffect*') in the first line, which as a result even sounds 'affected'.

Then, on the graphological level, the inverted commas round the phrase 'beyond her' appear to confirm the son's suspicion that his mother's mispronunciation of words that do not come naturally to her is quite deliberate, whereas on the same level the italics and misspelling of '*Bertold Brek*' are strongly suggestive of her wilful and confrontational pretence. This suggestion is further reinforced by the name's syntactic and prosodic isolation from the metrical line. It is, as it were, ostracized as alien. And, back again to the phonological level, had Brecht's name been pronounced as /brekt/, which is an acceptable alternative in English, it would have formed a perfect rhyme with 'affect', whereas /brek/ stands out as a disruption of the rhyme scheme, which perhaps is also suggestive of the mother's contrariness.

Another example of such linguistic anxiety is to be found in the sestet. In the lines preceding it, the mother keeps feigning ignorance out of loyalty to her roots and, in ostentatiously ungrammatical English, admonishes her son challengingly for having caused the estrangement between them: 'You/Know all them things'. As a token of filial love, he gives in and curbs his language, but notice how (the arrows indicate a feature of the metre which I will take up presently):

So I governed my tongue →
In front of her, a genuinely well- → → →
Adjusted adequate betrayal → →
Of what I knew better. I'd *naw* and *aye* →
And decently relapse into the wrong → →
Grammar which kept us allied and at bay.

We see in these lines that the predominance of Latinate words such as 'governed', 'genuinely', 'adjusted', 'adequate', 'betrayal', 'decently', and 'relapse', the lexical complexity, the convoluted syntax and its distribution across the metrical lines, provide a pointed representation of the mystifying double-speak in which the son expresses his undoubtedly well-intentioned attempt at self-denial: 'a genuinely well-/Adjusted adequate betrayal/Of what I knew better'. It is the typical ambivalent style of the intellectual revealing an almost obsessive need to save face. At the same time, the son's hedging and side-stepping language echoes the earlier account of his mother's 'fear of affectation', not only in terms of its laborious formulation but also by verbal repetition ('well-adjusted') and the use of related lexical items ('inadequacy', 'inadequate', 'adequate', 'betray', and 'betrayal').

The wording of his ultimate self-effacement is just as equivocal: 'I'd *naw* and *aye*/And decently relapse into the wrong/Grammar which kept us allied and at bay.' Considering that the verb 'relapse' has negative denotations and connotations, in that it is normally used in the sense of 'falling back, after an improvement, into a way of behaving that is undesirable', we might conclude that the son experiences his sacrifice as really degrading. If this inference is correct, the adverb 'decently' may be the cause of some tension between the subject 'I' and the predicate 'relapse into the wrong grammar'. This is because in this syntactic position 'decently' may be seen as both an attitudinal adverb and as an adverb of manner. Therefore, this ambiguity allows us to interpret the clause as 'I was so decent (i.e. polite, nice, courteous) as to relapse into the wrong grammar' and as 'I relapsed into the wrong grammar and did so decently (i.e. politely, nicely, courteously)'. In either case there seems to be an ironic mismatch between the words 'decently' and 'relapse'.

Yet another interesting point is the absence of a comma after the noun 'grammar' in the focused front position in the last line. This absence indicates that the modifying relative clause 'which kept us allied and at bay' is restricted to and essential for the identification of the antecedent noun 'grammar'. Significantly, this reveals that it is not the ambivalent act of self-denial, but 'the wrong grammar' which, paradoxically, keeps mother and son united and at odds.

In the linguistic **texture** of the poem, the tortuous features of the son's language appear to be enhanced on the interacting levels of syntax and phonology. We might notice how the grammatical structure of these two sentences of the sestet does not coincide with their metrical structure. Thus, the grammar of both sentences begins in the middle of a metrical line, while it also goes beyond no fewer than five metrical boundaries at line-ends. It is particularly in these places that the effects of the interplay between grammar and metre may have a marked impact.

We might say that in the case of enjambment, readers get two conflicting prompts: the metrical line-boundary tells them to pause, while the unfinished syntax pulls them into the next line. Therefore, however brief it may be, the resulting vacillation is bound to cause some tension, which, on the one hand, heightens our awareness of the last word in the enjambed line and, on the other, causes us to wonder about the first word in the next line. Obviously, poets may be expected to make the most of the manifold effects of enjambment, be it to the surprise, frustration, or amusement of the reader.

It should furthermore be noted that the acuteness of this tension is variable because it is related to the force of the syntactic pull at the line-end. This pull may be stronger or weaker, dependent on where in the syntactic hierarchy of words, phrases, and clauses the cut is made. Thus, enjambment between parts of words is relatively rare and is felt to be extremely forceful. You will have noted that there is one instance of such a severe enjambment in the poem, namely 'well-/Adjusted' in lines 10–11.

The force of enjambment between parts of phrases is generally experienced as variable. For instance, a cut between a modifying adverb and a following adjective ('too/Well-adjusted' in lines 6–7) would probably be felt to be slightly stronger than a break between two parts of a verb phrase ('whenever it came to/Pronouncing words' in lines 2–3), a break between a noun and a following modifier ('betrayal/Of what I knew better' in lines 11–12), or a break between an adjective and a noun ('the wrong/Grammar' in lines 15–16).

From this it follows that in the case of enjambment between relatively independent syntactic units, and between complete phrases and clauses, the pull at the end of the poetic line is usually experienced as least strong, though readers may also associate all kinds of representational meanings with this type of discordance. The poem contains the following instances of this kind of enjambment: between a verb and its object ('affect/Inadequacy' in lines 1–2, and 'betray/The hampered and inadequate' in lines 5–6), right before an independent adverb phrase ('... askew/Every time' in lines 4–5, and '...tongue/In front of her' in lines 9–10), and between two clauses ('I'd *naw* and *aye*/And decently relapse...' in lines 12–13).

By means of a single, a double, and a triple arrow I have marked, albeit tentatively, the relative difference in strength of the syntactic pull in the lines of the sestet. As I feel it, the tensions arising from this pattern of enjambments seem to reinforce the tension-ridden language of the son's gesture of submission and reconciliation, perhaps reflecting at the same time the tensions generated by the internal conflict between his professional pride and his filial love and respect.

Literary interpretation revisited

As I hope to have demonstrated, stylistic analysis can serve to substantiate the impressions of literary effect. Furthermore the focusing on specific features of language can lead us to wider issues of literary significance. One such issue is that of **intertextuality**, the way particular expressions recur in different texts and so provide a link between them. Consider, for example, the expression in line 9 of the poem, 'I governed my tongue'. This in the poem's context is likely to be rendered as 'I controlled or checked my language', or perhaps even as 'I kept a civil tongue in my head'. However, there is more to it than that because the wording of the clause appears to produce echoes from Heaney's earlier work.

The alternative reality represented in poetry is a function of the interaction between its linguistic features and the ideas, experiences, and emotions of the individual reader. It therefore stands to reason that the intellectual and emotional baggage we bring with us when reading a particular text will also contain remembered and half-remembered snatches or longer passages from other texts we have read. These texts in turn will have their own intertextual dimensions, and so it goes on endlessly. Obviously, the texts in such an intertextual network may be related to each other for all sorts of reasons. Topical coherence may be one of them: this book, for instance, is related to a maze of other texts which are, in different ways, concerned with stylistics. Another strong bond between texts may be **genre**. Thus, literary texts may be related through a specific genre and, in the case of this Heaney poem, our interpretation depends to a degree on the associations we make with the traditional formality of the sonnet.

To return to the clause 'I governed my tongue'. This can be said to derive additional significance from its intertextual relation with Heaney's collection of essays, *The Government of the Tongue*, published in 1989. This title, we should note, is ambiguous and rakes up an old controversy: should the tongue (which for Heaney represents both the common resources of language and the poet's personal gift of utterance) be governed or should it be the governor? It is the conflict between art's isolation and participation, between its artistic autonomy and ideological dependence, and in particular between poetry and the established social order. In his book, Heaney characterizes poetry in the following way:

> The fact is that poetry is its own reality and no matter how much a poet may concede to the corrective pressures of social, moral, political and historical reality, the ultimate fidelity must be to the demands and promise of the artistic event. (page 101)

This closely parallels the notion of literature as representation which has been proposed in this book. The question arises as to whether Heaney lived up to this credo when writing the sonnet in memory of his mother. How far does the textual design of the poem that we have been scrutinizing achieve the artistic fidelity he refers to here?

As was pointed out earlier in the chapter, the first impression we get of the poem is of verbal clumsiness, of something 'almost breathtakingly ill-made', and so lacking, it would seem, in artistic craft. Thus, on the phonological level, the sonnet's rhyme-scheme is relatively consistent, but at what price to the rhyming words themselves? One would think that no self-respecting poet would come up with clumsy rhymes like 'to'/'too'/'you', 'tongue'/'wrong', and 'well'/'betrayal'. And to make things worse, on the combined level of syntax and phonology, these words stand out because they are, be it momentarily, foregrounded at the enjambed line-ends. Moreover, as we have seen, they are also the cause of some strained syntactic overflows, which makes a smooth reading rather difficult. On yet another level of linguistic structure, the high measure of lexical repetition seems out of proportion, especially considering the relatively small space of a sonnet. Furthermore, in this undeniably emotive context, the dominant use of Latinate words is quite uncommon because they are generally associated with greater formality, abstraction, and emotional neutrality, whereas English words of Germanic, i.e. Anglo-Saxon, origin are generally associated with things which are fundamental, familiar, concrete, or emotional in our lives.

On the other hand, it is hard to believe that a Nobel Prize-winning poet could have made 'something hampered and askew', particularly not for such an occasion. So when the formal patterns in the poem, whether ungainly or not, seem to yield representational effects, one begins to assume that the poem is clumsy by design, in both senses of that term, and that it is intrinsic to the poet's fidelity to 'the demands and promise of the artistic event'. With this in mind, we might also speculate about the additional intertextual significance of the 'unwieldy' lines 'So I governed my tongue/In front of her, a genuinely well-/Adjusted adequate betrayal/Of what I knew better'. Perhaps the clause 'I governed my tongue' may not only be rendered as 'I curbed my language' but also as 'I curbed my poetic gift'. If this is so, the poet has indeed made the supreme sacrifice of 'betraying' his profession to restore the union with his mother, while, paradoxically, his poem turns out to be a splendid artistic representation of a touching tribute to her memory.

Conclusion

In previous chapters, I used literary texts to illustrate how various features of style can be subjected to linguistic analysis. In this chapter we have focused attention on the interpretation of a complete poetic text and tried to show how stylistics can lend support to literary critical appreciation by providing further substantiation of significance. It is important to note that there is no claim that such analysis provides the means of arriving at a definitive interpretation, but only that it enables readers to adduce textual evidence for their own sense of what the poem means to them. Stylistics in no way replaces literary appreciation, but simply serves to bring it into clearer focus.

With the exception of three non-literary texts in the first three chapters, our main concern has been with literary texts, and these have been submitted to a stylistic analysis focused entirely on the interpretation of the individual reader. In Chapter 7 we will take up the question of how far stylistic analysis might be applied in support of a social reading process of literary texts in which the reader is ideologically positioned. Since this leads on to the question as to whether, from this sociocultural and political perspective, there remains sufficient basis for distinguishing literary and non-literary texts, we end this survey as we started it, with some newspaper headlines, though this time our analysis will be from a different viewpoint.

7
Stylistics and ideological perspectives

The discussion so far in this book has focused largely on the individual interpretation of literary texts. We have sought to demonstrate how stylistic analysis can direct attention to specific linguistic features in a text and so provide textual substantiation for the different kinds of literary effect it might have on the reader. We have argued that this literary effect is a matter of realizing the potential in the text for creating new contexts and representing alternative realities. Needless to say, we bring to this process of realization the whole gamut of cognitive and emotive experiences we have built up in the course of our personal lives, which in turn generates an individual—and thereby always divergent—reading.

But individuality is also a social construct: it develops in response to, or in reaction to, various sociocultural influences. Individuals are also members of social groups of various kinds. Their response to literary texts is necessarily influenced by the sociocultural values and beliefs that define these groups, in short by their ideologies. One could accordingly shift emphasis and consider how interpretation is informed by such ideologies. This is what is done, for example, in literary criticism informed by Marxist, feminist, and post-colonialist perspectives, the main aim of which is, in broad terms, to relate the understanding and interpretation of literary texts to particular sociocultural, economic, and political contexts in the present and the past. These theories have produced revisions of traditional critical readings of canonical texts, arguing that these traditional readings are not neutral but are themselves implicitly ideological. By the same token, they have raised questions about the exclusiveness of the literary canon itself, and have argued for the inclusion of hitherto suppressed or neglected groups of authors, for example, working-class and women writers, African-American writers, and those representative of other minorities.

Social reading and ideological positioning

We have already talked about perspective as expressed through literary texts. Here we are concerned with it as an ideological positioning of the reader, and its effect on interpretation. This shift from an individual to a social reading reveals all kinds of possible significance which would otherwise be unnoticed. To take just one example. You can read the novels of Charles Dickens and appreciate their dramatic descriptions, their intricacy of plot, their colourful characterization, but if you turn a critical eye to their underlying ideological significance, it becomes apparent that what is represented as the desirable norm of goodness and virtue is associated with middle-class values. Whatever trials and tribulations the heroes go through, their rehabilitation at the end is achieved by being restored to bourgeois respectability. And the central figures are indeed predominantly heroes, not heroines. There are plenty of women in the novels, it is true, but they tend to play a supporting and subordinate role, their purpose being to set off the features of the men. Those characters who do not have hero status tend to be polarized as good or evil, and are often idiosyncratic in appearance or behaviour. The only 'normal' people are the heroes: the custodians of the desired social norm.

Once our attention is drawn to the potential ideological significance of literary texts, we become sensitized to the possibility of alternative readings linked to sociopolitical values. So it is that Marxist and feminist critics, for example, have produced revisionist interpretations and re-evaluations of literary works which are of great interest. It is worth noting that their ability to do this is again indicative of how the disconnectedness of the literary text naturally gives rise to a diversity of discourses. The alternative realities which the ideologically committed critic reads into the text are of a social rather than individual kind, but this does not make them any more definite or authoritative: they are partial and literary interpretations all the same.

The example of Charles Dickens' novels, cited above, shows how ideological interpretation can apply to macro aspects of fiction like character and plot. But it can also apply to the fine-grained stylistic analysis which we are concerned with in this book. A simple example or two. Here are some lines from Alexander Pope's poem 'Epistle to a Lady: Of the Characters of Women':

243   See how the World its Veterans rewards!
        A Youth of frolicks, an old Age of Cards,
245   Fair to no purpose, artful to no end,
        Young without Lovers, old without a Friend,
        A Fop their Passion, but their Prize a Sot,
248   Alive, ridiculous, and dead, forgot!

We may admire the verbal craft with which these lines are composed and substantiate our admiration with stylistic comment. We might, for example, note the way the textual patterns develop in lines 244–6 through a series of phrases in which grammatical equivalences co-occur with lexical contrasts; how line 247 disrupts the pattern by subtly reversing the structure, and how the pattern is then reasserted in the following line with particular force with four directly juxtaposed lexical items resounding like the chords of a musical phrase, and ending the passage with a kind of emphatic finality. We might further note how this last line is more emotionally charged, and how the disturbance in line 247 of the symmetrical patterning of lines 244–6 seems to mark a shift from rational detachment to an expression of contempt, only just held in check by the compressed pattern of the line. So much for the aesthetic appreciation of Pope's lines. But we need also to note that all this verbal craft is directed at the denigration of women. The poem represents a dismissively negative stereotype of the female character, a projection of male prejudice, and the very artistry of the lines makes this negative representation all the more effective. We may admire the verbal art but deplore what it represents.

In the case of these lines by Pope, the ideological position of the poet is plain, indeed blatant. In other cases it is less obvious and one can argue that it is the purpose of analysis to bring it out. Consider, for example, the poem by John Betjeman that was discussed in Chapter 3. In my reading of the poem, the wife's role is deeply moving and entirely in keeping with what one might expect in such a dreadful and hopeless situation. Her timid self-effacement, the futility of her actions and banality of her words are authentic representations of the bitter realization of her desperate helplessness and painful inadequacy. These are emotions anybody, irrespective of sex, can identify with. However, from the point of view of **feminist stylistics**, it might well be argued that this is the **dominant reading** of the text. In other words, this reading is not to be seen as the writer's intention, which is unknowable anyway, but as the one that appears to be the most obvious and natural because it is upheld by the dominant ideologies about the role of women in the society of the time (the poem was first published in 1954). Just because this position that the poem offers to the reader is found to be most commonsensical, even women may be drawn into endorsing its underlying ideologies. On the other hand, as we have said repeatedly, the meaning of a text is not intrinsic to it, but always negotiable. Therefore, feminist readers are enabled to criticize the dominant reading and construct an alternative reading in which the habitualized assumptions about the position of women are exposed and rejected. In fact, in feminist stylistics such a **resistant reading** is seen as a suitable starting point for a description focusing on other elements of the text that might produce an analysis and interpretation along the following lines.

There are two people in the poem, a man and a woman, and in our discussion in Chapter 3 we demonstrated how the description represents the man's perspective. It is the reality of his experience that we are drawn into. 'His wife stands timidly by': she is set aside. Inanimate features of the scene are described, but she is not. Of the two, she is the only one who actually does anything (the rest of the poem is about the man's state of mind) but we note that her only action is 'She puts her fingers in his'. This is described as 'loving and silly', and in the context of the man's distress appears to be superficial and inadequate. And her superficiality seems to be further borne out by what she says. In the poem there are two examples of speech and thought representation. It is clear that the first expresses not what the man actually says, but the kind of thoughts that are running through his head:

'Oh merciless, hurrying Londoners! Why was I made
   For the long and the painful deathbed coming to me?'

The second example appears contrastively in a parallel position
in the following, and last, verse. This is in direct speech (DS) and
gives us the wife's actual words. And very trivial and humdrum
words they are too:

'It's cheaper to take the tube to Piccadilly
   And then we can catch a nineteen or a twenty-two.'

So it is easy to see that we could give all this a sexist gloss. The
wife stands timidly by, not involved, but marginalized. It is the
man's sensations and emotions that are represented and that we
are drawn into identifying with. She, on the contrary, is shown to
be capable only of a superficial response.

Having looked at poetry as a site of questionable **ideology**, we
shall now turn to a piece of prose fiction. It is an extract from
Chapter 6 of George Eliot's novel *The Mill on the Floss*, and
describes the scene in which Tom and Maggie have to share a
third remaining jam-puff:

... the knife descended on the puff and it was in two, but the
result was not satisfactory to Tom, for he still eyed the halves
doubtfully. At last he said,
'Shut your eyes, Maggie.'
'What for?'
'You never mind what for. Shut 'em when I tell you.'
Maggie obeyed.
'Now, which'll you have Maggie — right hand or left?'
'I'll have that with the jam run out,' said Maggie, keeping her
eyes shut to please Tom.
'Why, you don't like that, you silly. You may have it if it
comes to you fair, but I shan't give it you without. Right or
left — you choose, now. Ha-a-a!' said Tom, in a tone of exasperation, as Maggie peeped. 'You keep your eyes shut, now,
else you shan't have any.'
Maggie's power of sacrifice did not extend so far, indeed I
fear she cared less that Tom should enjoy the utmost possible
amount of puff than that he should be pleased with her for

giving him the best bit. So she shut her eyes quite close, till Tom told her to 'say which,' and then she said, 'Left-hand.'

'You've got it,' said Tom, in rather a bitter tone.

'What, the bit with the jam run out?'

'No: here, take it,' said Tom firmly, handing decidedly the best piece to Maggie.

'O, please, Tom, have it: I don't mind—I like the other: please take this.'

'No, I shan't,' said Tom, almost crossly, beginning on his own inferior piece.

Maggie, thinking it was no use to contend further, began too, and ate up her half-puff with considerable relish as well as rapidity. But Tom had finished first, and had to look on while Maggie ate her last morsel or two, feeling in himself a capacity for more. Maggie didn't know Tom was looking at her: she was seesawing on the elder bough, lost to almost everything but a vague sense of jam and idleness.

'O, you greedy thing!' said Tom, when she had swallowed the last morsel. He was conscious of having acted very fairly, and thought she ought to have considered this and made up to him for it. He would have refused a bit of hers beforehand, but one is naturally at a different point of view before and after one's own share of puff is swallowed.

Maggie turned quite pale. 'O Tom, why didn't you ask me?'

'*I* wasn't going to ask you for a bit, you greedy. You might have thought of it without, when you knew I gave you the best bit.'

'But I wanted you to have it—you know I did,' said Maggie in an injured tone.

'Yes, but I wasn't going to do what wasn't fair, like Spouncer. He always takes the best bit, if you don't punch him for it, and if you choose the best with your eyes shut, he changes his hands. But if I go halves I'll go 'em fair—only I wouldn't be a greedy.' [Here Tom abruptly breaks off the talk and starts to play with his dog.]

But Maggie, gifted with that superior power of misery which distinguishes the human being and places him at a proud distance from the most melancholy chimpanzee, sat still on her bough, and gave herself up to the keen sense of unmerited reproach. She would have given the world not to have eaten all her puff, and to have saved some of it for Tom.

As a sensitive representation of the relationship between these two children, sister and brother, I find this passage deeply human and extremely moving. But, of course, one could also take an **ideological perspective** and read into it a prefiguration of the typical male–female differences in ways of behaving and speaking in adult relationships, because these differences, feminist linguists claim, have already begun in early childhood. Girls and boys, even those who have been brought up in the same family, like sisters and brothers, grow up in different worlds with different behaviours and different languages. Observational studies have shown that, in their play world, boys give orders, are overbearing, and are prepared to use physical force to get what they want. Their games have winners and losers and complex rules they constantly argue about. This is because they tend to play in large hierarchical peer groups in which status can only be gained after a lot of in-fighting. In their world, girls also want to get their way, but go about it differently. They do not give orders, but put forward ideas, which are more easily accepted; they seek to compromise, and do not openly aspire to status. Since they seek intimacy, they usually play in smaller groups or in pairs, and many of their games have no winners and losers. Their main concern is to be liked.

The way Tom and Maggie go about sharing the jam-puff is a perfect illustration of the socially determined clash between the behaviours and conversational styles of boys and girls as set out above. So a feminist reading might suggest that Maggie's 'superior power of misery' reveals not so much the difference between human beings and chimpanzees as that between the different sexes of human beings. It will see these characters not as individuals but as types—even stereotypes—of male and female roles, perhaps almost as typical social positions rather than individual persons. However, I would read the passage as the representation of tension between individual characters and be drawn into sympathy with Maggie as an exploited person.

As was pointed out earlier, it is of the very nature of literature that it gives rise to diverse interpretations, and once alerted to the possibility of reading ideological significance into a text, we can, of course interrogate any work of literature along these lines. Such an approach is salutary in that it challenges conventional certainties. But it also brings up the difficult issue of the relationship between aesthetic and moral judgements. How far is a literary work to be preferred or rejected on the grounds of the kind of reality it represents? To what extent should a commitment to a particular sociopolitical position explicitly inform stylistic analysis and the critical evaluation of literary works?

Incorporation of literary criticism into linguistic criticism?

The adoption of a social perspective is based on the belief that literary texts can be construed as verbalizations of sociocultural and political values. But then all texts are verbalizations of this kind: advertisements, newspaper reports, guidebooks, promotional pamphlets, and so on. All of them can be construed as social documents in which ideological positions are implicitly or explicitly expressed. Two consequences would seem to follow from this social perspective on literature. The first is that there is no essential difference between literary and non-literary texts in that both are expressions of social reality. The distinction between **representation** and **reference** that was drawn earlier in this book will therefore become null and void. The second consequence is that the stylistic procedures of close analysis will be indistinguishable, no matter whether they are applied to literary or non-literary texts. Similarly, *literary* criticism as such ceases to exist, and is incorporated into **linguistic criticism**, which seeks to draw out the social significance of all textual practices.

Critical discourse analysis (CDA)

We have, in fact, already discussed such a 'general purpose' type of stylistics in Chapter 1, where we talked about style in general, and demonstrated with reference to a newspaper headline and a publisher's blurb the significance of linguistic choice for the interpretation of non-literary texts. Then, in Chapter 3, we expanded our earlier textual analysis of the headline by relating its marked linguistic forms to a relevant context of social practice, in this case the sociocultural situation of a British national newspaper and its readers. In doing so, we treated the headline as **discourse**. What we did not do, however, was to 'politicize' this discourse by assuming that linguistic choices in texts—in all texts—are, consciously or unconsciously, motivated by particular value systems and beliefs, and that the resulting discourses are therefore always presented from some ideological perspective. This politicization is the business of what is variously called Critical Language Study, Critical Linguistics, or **critical discourse analysis**. In what follows I will use the last-mentioned term, or its usual abbreviation, **CDA**.

The epithet 'critical' implies revealing how conventional uses of language are imbued with ideological positions of which, more often than not, many people are not aware. They have lost this awareness as a result of constant exposure to dominant norms, value-systems, and beliefs which are linguistically mediated in the discourses of powerful political, social, and cultural institutions such as the government, the law, education, the press, and the world of advertising. To put it differently, by constantly hammering at the same themes, the massive publicity output of these institutions has induced the majority of people to see their ideological positions as normal, even to the extent of regarding them as matters of mere common sense.

Consider, for example, how literally millions of readers of the British tabloid newspaper *The Sun* are day by day exposed to the discursive practice of representing women in terms of discriminatory stereotypes. The following is a small selection from the issue of July 31, 2001:

'the excited Welsh blonde', 'crimper Helen', 'the bubbly blonde', 'chirpy Helen', 'bitchy Narinder', 'busty Dawn, 20', 'busty newlywed Dawn Wilson', 'lovecheat Dawn', (her married partner in a love affair is called 'Dirty Bertie Gotobed, 47', one of the very few discrediting names referring to a man), 'sobbing Joan Falconio', 'Terri Thigh-er' (a pun on her real name Terri Dwyer?), 'the leggy blonde', 'bikini-clad babes', 'glamour model Jordan'

Having developed an unconscious knowledge of discourse types, some readers, when this dormant awareness is roused, might be prepared to admit that most of these qualifications could not possibly be used to represent men. So the discriminatory naming is not a property of the language as text but as discourse, that is, how the language is *used* in the wide context of British society. Even if these, and similar, ways of describing women are not intended as discrimination, the fact remains that this daily bombardment of stereotyping expressions is most likely to reinforce the dominant ideology, which may even have hardened into a common-sense idea, that women belong to a distinct gender category.

British newspapers are also a boundless source of (usually concealed) political ideologies. Thus, a critical linguist might well be intrigued by the following headlines:

> WAKE UP, EU LOT
> PM's modernise or fail ultimatum to fellow leaders
> (*The Sun*, July 31, 2001)

> REFORM OR EUR DOOMED
> Blair tells EU to get in shape for euro
> (*The Mirror*, July 31, 2001)

My first impression is that one does not even need to read the news stories themselves to surmise that these headlines are not so much concerned with Mr Blair's plea for economic reforms in the European Union as with the emotional and divisive issue of Britain signing up to the single currency, the euro, on which even a referendum might be held.

In each case the large print of the primary headline actually reinforces the shouting peremptory tone of their imperative grammatical structure, with *The Mirror* sounding like a fire-and-brimstone sermon, and *The Sun* like a duty-sergeant's early morning call. In addition to these intertextual echoes, both headlines appeal to the reader's awareness of sound associations: both exploit phonetic similarities, 'EUR' and 'you're', and 'EU' and 'you' respectively.

More seriously, as a result of these linguistic devices, common in tabloids and used to relate to the reader, both headlines represent a speaking voice. This raises the question of whose voice we are hearing, and therewith whose perspective is adopted. Also, who is being addressed? The actual voices, and therewith the perspectives, are of course those of the two newspapers, but the rhetorical tricks we have just described may well induce many readers to overlook this, and to make the newspaper's perspective their own. The question of who is being addressed is highly ambivalent. The obvious thing to say is that the actual addressees are the readers, but that they will interpret the message of the headlines as being aimed at the European Union. However, because of the phonetic ambiguity of 'EUR'/'you're' and 'EU'/'you', the headlines, if read as 'Reform or you're doomed' and 'Wake up, you lot', may just as well be interpreted as an urgent appeal to the readers to think twice before they say yes to an euro-referendum or put their trust in a government that will make Britain join the Euro-zone.

What, then, are the political perspectives of these two tabloids that they want their millions of readers to share? It seems that their political convictions are strongly infected by nationalistic sentiments. These feelings prompt the idea that Britain is superior to any other nation, and that these other nations will only fare better if they do what Britain tells them to do. This is borne out by the secondary headlines in which 'Blair tells EU to get in shape' and issues an 'ultimatum' to his fellow leaders. Again, the wording of these secondary headlines is probably a far cry from what Mr Blair actually said, and is no more than wishful thinking.

It seems to me that CDA's commitment to expose the way in which language in use mediates a usually hidden ideological representation of the world is salutary. However, looking back at my own attempt at a critical discourse analysis, I wonder if it is not too much biased by my own political perspective, which might very well result in an imbalance between analysis and interpretation. This problem also brings to mind the position of readers in CDA. If they are not equipped to deal with the ideologically loaded discourses they encounter in daily life, how will they cope with the ideological biases of critical discourse analysts? In CDA, are readers just passive receptacles, or are they active agents, producing their own representations? As I hope I have made clear in this book, the latter is the way in which readers are regarded in literary stylistics.

Conclusion

With this final question, it appears that this survey of stylistics has come full circle. In it I have tried to indicate how a close attention to specific linguistic features of text can serve not only to substantiate an impressionistic sense of meaning, but also to suggest the possibilities of reading different interpretations into a text, of both an individual and a social significance. Perhaps the most important claim that can be made for stylistics is that its very precision of analysis reveals how divergent and various the effects of different features of style can be. It shows up how the very richness of language as a resource for making meaning makes this meaning unstable, uncertain, and in the last analysis, elusive.

Readings

Chapter 1
The concept of style

Text 1

GRAHAM HOUGH: *Style and Stylistics*. Routledge & Kegan Paul 1969, pages 1–4

The modern study of style, i.e. stylistics, has its roots in classical rhetoric: the ancient art of persuasive speech, which has always had a close affinity with literature, probably because it was regarded as a persuasive discourse, too. As is pointed out in this text, classical rhetoric was prescriptive in that it provided guidance as to how to be persuasive, whereas modern stylistics is descriptive in that it seeks to point out the linguistic features that can be associated with particular effects.

It is a paradox that the term 'style' has tended to disappear from the main stream of modern criticism, while a quasi-independent study of 'stylistics' has simultaneously made its appearance. ...

The concept of style is an old one; it goes back to the very beginnings of literary thought in Europe. It appears in connection with rhetoric rather than poetic, and there seems to be no special reason for this, except that style is regarded as part of the technique of persuasion and therefore discussed largely under the head of oratory. Ancient rhetoric distinguished between ceremonial, political and forensic oratory, and each has its own appropriate occasion and appropriate repertory of devices. If you wish to produce *this* particular effect *these* are the means to bring it about; the proper vocabulary, type of syntax and figures of speech can be prescribed for the purpose in hand (Aristotle, *Rhetoric*, Bk. III; Quintilian, *Institutes of Oratory*, Bk. VIII). The tone of this ancient rhetoric is largely prescriptive—the giving of instructions for appropriate and effective composition. ... Ancient rhetoric in its later phases tended to enlarge its discussion to historians and other prose writers. In the Middle Ages and the Renaissance this immense body of rhetorical precept was largely incorporated into poetic, where it had a deep influence not only on critical ideas, but, as recent studies have shown, on the composition of poetry itself. The tradition carries on a lingering existence even into the eighteenth century.

But for us all this is a vanished history. Prescriptive criticism has not been a central literary activity for the last 300 years. In a post-Romantic age it survives only in odd corners—schools of journalism, classes in 'creative writing'. Modern literary study does not presume to dictate to poets; it does not offer instructions towards the forming of a style, it examines styles that are already formed. It is parallel in this respect to linguistic study, which no longer lays down rules for correct grammar, but studies the rules that are actually adhered to by particular cultural groups. The aim is not to give laws for human utterance, but to understand the utterances that actually occur.

▷ *Why do you think Hough calls stylistics a 'quasi-independent' study?*

▷ *Hough does not seem to think very highly of classes in 'creative writing'. Do you think that stylistics might in principle have a role to play in such classes?*

Text 2
DWIGHT BOLINGER: *Aspects of Language* (2nd edn.). Harcourt Brace Jovanovich 1975, pages 600–1

The following text raises the old question as to whether we can or cannot make a distinction between the message (what is said) and the form it takes (how it is said).

...what do we mean by style? Common to all definitions is the notion that 'Y is used in place of X, where both X and Y are practically the same.' Style involves a choice of form without a change of message. It involves that, but of course it is more than that. It includes the motives for the choice and its effects. Often these are impossible to distinguish from the content. If a writer wants to convey a supernatural presence and chooses words with phones-thematic supernatural overtones rather than synonyms without them, has he made a stylistic choice or a semantic one? If all differences in form are correlated with differences in meaning, then the style of a piece of writing is simply its meaning. The work may stand out because of its meaning, or the author may be exceptionally skilled in finding the right words for his meaning and we take pleasure in his art, but the wrong choices would have meant something less—they would not have conveyed the meaning. Style and meaning are inseparable.

▷ *'Style involves a choice of form without a change of message. …but…it is much more than that.' So what else is involved?*

▷ *Can you think of examples where a different choice of form would greatly change the message and where it would not?*

▷ *If 'style and meaning are inseparable', does it follow that we can never say the 'same thing' in different words?*

Text 3

ELIZABETH CLOSS TRAUGOTT and MARY LOUISE PRATT: *Linguistics for Students of Literature.* Harcourt Brace Jovanovich 1980, pages 29–30

This text also discusses the question of style and meaning but does so in terms of the relationship between two kinds of meaning: semantic meaning which is encoded in the language itself, and pragmatic meaning which is achieved in context.

Stylistic choice is usually regarded as a matter of form or expression, that is, as choice among different ways of expressing an invariant or predetermined content. But this view is misleading, for writers obviously choose content too. In our grammar, with its semantic and pragmatic components, both content and expression can be viewed as matters of choice. Choice of content involves choice of semantic structures; choice of expression involves choice of pragmatic functions and contextual features (such as what relation a speaker adopts towards the hearer, what inferences are to be conveyed, what assumptions made). Choices in both these components of the grammar are in turn the basis for phonological, syntactic, and lexical choices. This approach provides us with a new way of thinking about whether there is or is not a duality between form and content. This issue has been discussed in philosophy and aesthetics for centuries. A large number of critics and stylisticians acknowledge such a duality, saying that given some particular content ('meaning') a variety of surface forms are possible. In this view it is possible for there to be sentences that are synonymous, even though they have different forms. The opposing position is that every difference in form brings a difference in meaning and that synonymy is therefore impossible. Now it is clearly useful to say that MY TWENTY-THREE YEAR OLD BROTHER IS A BACHELOR is synonymous with (has the same meaning as) MY TWENTY-THREE YEAR OLD BROTHER IS UNMARRIED. Yet they are not exactly equivalent. For example, one would scarcely say the first sentence to a child because 'bachelor' is a technical term, while one might say the second. The difference is pragmatic, not semantic. In terms of our grammar, in choosing between these two sentences, the speaker makes a pragmatic, contextually motivated choice between two semantically equivalent surface forms. Thus the grammar allows for synonymy (thereby maintaining a form/content distinction) and at the same time accounts for the fact that synonymous forms are not exactly equivalent.

▷ *'This approach provides us with a new way of thinking about whether there is or is not a duality between form and content.' What is this new way of thinking? Are the authors arguing for such a duality or against it? How is their way of thinking different from that expressed in Text 2?*

▷ *The author of Text 2 talks about the difficulty of distinguishing between a 'stylistic choice' and a 'semantic one'. The authors of this text talk about 'choice of content' as distinct from 'choice of expression'. Are they talking about the same thing?*

▷ *The authors talk about style as involving 'a pragmatic, contextually motivated choice between two semantically equivalent surface forms'. Do you think this is a satisfactory way of accounting for the difference between the two headlines discussed in Section 1, Chapter 7?*

▷ What 'semantically equivalent surface forms' could you suggest in a rewriting of the blurb in Section 1, Chapter 1 in a different style?

Chapters 2 and 3
Style in literature: Text and discourse

Text 4
RONALD CARTER: *Keywords in Language and Literacy*. Routledge 1995, page 155

Texts 4 and 5 deal with the concepts of 'text' and 'discourse'. Though the terms have gained wide currency, there is no general agreement about their exact meaning and application.

[Text] is a term commonly used by linguists to refer to a complete stretch of language, either spoken or written. A one-line advertisement or headline can be a text since it is a complete semantic unit, but the practice of text analysis (also known as text linguistics) is not principally concerned with individual words or sentences. It is concerned with the way in which they combine across sentence boundaries and speaking turns to form coherently organised language in use in a specific context. ...

It should also be recognised that the term 'text' often refers to a definable communicative unit with a clearly discernible social or cultural function. Thus a casual conversation, a sermon, a poster, a poem, or an advertisement would be referred to as texts. In some studies in this field, the terms 'text' and 'text analysis' can be interchangeable with 'discourse' and 'discourse analysis'.

The term 'text' in the sense of a unit of spoken and written material to be analysed and criticised has a particular ascendancy at present in the field of English Studies, which was previously dominated by a study of literary 'works'. Depending on one's position, the term 'text' either serves to democratise English Studies so that no one type of text is unduly privileged, or it serves to undermine the critical judgements of the past, which have established a canon of literary works deemed to be of lasting value within and beyond the national culture that produced them.

▷ *In what respect are the definitions of 'text' given here different from that in Section 1, Chapter 3?*

▷ *How could the term 'text' serve to 'democratize' English Studies? And how could it serve to undermine the canonization of literary works?*

Text 5

KATIE WALES: *A Dictionary of Stylistics* (2nd edn.). Pearson Education 2001, pages 113–15

Discourse is one of the most widely used and overworked terms in many branches of linguistics, stylistics, cultural and critical theory....

Its technical uses appear to have really little to do with the senses recorded in the *COD* [*Concise Oxford Dictionary*], for instance: namely a formal written 'treatise' or 'dissertation'; or (archaically) 'talk' or 'conversation'...

One prominent and comprehensive sense, for which there is indeed no other direct equivalent, covers all those aspects of communication which involve not only a message or text but also the addresser and addressee, and their immediate context of situation. Leech and Short ([*Style in Fiction*], 1981), emphasize its interpersonal or transactional nature, and also its social purpose. Discourse would therefore refer not only to ordinary conversation and its context, but also to written communications between writer and reader: hence terms like literary or narrative discourse, discourse world, etc.... In this broad sense, discourse 'includes' text, but the two terms are not always easily distinguished, and are often used synonymously....

With the emphasis on communication in speech or writing it is often used simply as an alternative to variety or register: literary v. non-literary discourse, dramatic, philosophical, etc. And the terms discourse genre/type are now commonly used instead of register, for instance....

Discourse is popularly used in linguistics and literary theory in a more loaded sense after the work of Foucault. Discourse transmits social and institutionalized values or ideologies, and also creates them. Thus we can speak of the discourse of New Labour, of the tabloids, of regulations, etc. ... Foucault ([*The Archaeology of Knowledge*], 1972) also uses the term discursive practices as a general label for the larger discourse frameworks which reflect and inscribe sets of significant social, cultural and political beliefs at any one period: e.g. education, politics, information technology. Diachronically, we can see how one kind of discursive practice can come to eclipse another: e.g. currently 'New Age' philosophy over orthodox religion and medicine.

▷ *'In this broad sense, discourse "includes" text, but the two terms are not always easily distinguished, and are often used synonymously.' Does 'this broad sense' more or less square with the definition of the term 'discourse' in Section 1, Chapter 3? Why, do you think, did the author put the verb 'include' in scare-quotes?*

Text 6

ROGER FOWLER: *Literature as Social Discourse: The Practice of Linguistic Criticism.* Batsford Academic and Educational Ltd 1981, page 7

Fowler regards discourse as the expression of cultural and political values, and therefore socially determined. This includes literature, which is fully exposed to the forces of society like any other discourse.

I argue that, first and foremost, literature is a kind of *discourse*, a language activity within social structure like other forms of discourse. It is as amenable to linguistic study as are all other discourses such as conversations, letters, notices, book-writing, broadcasting, etc. Linguistic analysis of literary discourse aims first of all to specify the formal patterns of texts—poems, plays, novels, etc.—with a degree of precision which is unachievable in conventional literary criticism; avoiding impressionism and permitting clearly articulated debate. But the project goes further than just describing the formal structures which give texts their shape and texture. It is a mistake to regard literary texts as autonomous patterns of linguistic form cut off from social forces. If a linguist such as myself sees them as not simply *texts* but also, or rather, as *discourses*, all kinds of ways are open to interpret and describe them in terms of their vital cultural functions. From this perspective, literature is, like all language, interaction between people and between institutions and people. To regard it as social discourse is to stress its interpersonal and institutional dimensions, concentrating on those parts of textual structure which reflect and which influence relations within society. A study of literary styles which concentrates on such matters requires methodological and theoretical underpinnings which are more sophisticated and more ambitious than those usually presupposed in linguistic stylistics.

▷ *How far do you think Fowler's conception of discourse here agrees with that of Foucault as presented in Text 5?*

▷ *Do you agree that only the treatment of literature as 'social discourse' enables us to interpret and describe its vital cultural functions?*

Text 7
DAVID BIRCH: '"Working effects with words" — whose words?: Stylistics and reader intertextuality.' In Ronald Carter and Paul Simpson (eds.): *Language, Discourse and Literature: An Introductory Reader in Discourse Stylistics.* Unwin Hyman 1989, page 261

This text argues against a stylistics which assumes that meanings are located in the text instead of in the subjective reading of the analyst/reader in a particular social, cultural, and political context.

A stylistics predominantly concerned with static interpretation spends its time *recovering* meaning by close analysis of interrelated linguistic levels. This is an argument in support of maintaining the primacy of the writer (and the mythical static meaning supposedly encoded into the text by the writer), and as a consequence, in support of the whole literature discipline and literature machinery that judges what should and should not be read.... Such a stylistics produces some valuable insights, but they are insights related to a theoretical base which is, for me at any rate, wholly unsatisfactory. I prefer to work with a stylistics that is more focused on the semiotics of the production of meanings in social discourse, of which a text, determined by whatever means to be literary, is just a part, not the whole; a stylistics, then, which is rather more concerned with reading processes; a stylistics which is intertextual, instead of treating the text as an autonomous arte-fact labelled as intrinsically special by literary ideologues. This does not mean that this stylistics is simply a study of register, but that it is concerned with understanding literariness and intertext-uality as *a process of reading*, and with demythologizing notions of autonomy of text and 'poetic language' and that language, style, literary form and critic are innocent, disinterested and transparent vehicles for the expressing of meaning.

▷ *The author holds that a text-immanent stylistics is an argument in support of perpetuating 'the whole literature discipline and literature machinery that judges what should and should not be read...'. In what sense does this relate to the view expressed in Text 4 that the conception of 'text' as an umbrella term for all types of text may put an end to the privileged position in English Studies of literary 'works'?*

Text 8

GUY COOK: *Discourse and Literature: The Interplay of Form and Mind*. Oxford University Press 1994, pages 190–2

This text is concerned with identifying the distinctive features of kinds of discourse in reference to the concept of the schema. Schemata (schemas) are cultural constructs, conven-tional ways in which a community structures its reality. The text argues that some discourses, typically, but not exclusively of a literary kind, are designed to disrupt and reorganize such schemata.

Experience may be divided into three types: that which is per-ceived directly without the mediation of language (though it may also include language); that which comes to us entirely through language, but we believe represents an independent reality; and that which exists only through language, with no accessible cor-responding reality in the world, though it creates an illusion of one. Much literary discourse is of the last type. This is not only true of fiction. Even literary discourse derived from and representing independent 'facts' is unlikely to have the same immediate impact upon the reader as a discourse reporting a situation which directly affects the reader, or in which the reader can intervene. The boundaries here are fuzzy. Some discourses apparently derived from an independent reality (a memorandum, for example, or a summons to court), may directly involve their reader, while others (for example, newspaper reports), though also representing reality, may be so far beyond the reader's control or experience, that they are to all intents and purposes of the same status as the illusory world of a literary discourse. ...

Despite this fuzziness and complexity,... it seems reasonable to identify a group of texts of no immediate practical or social consequence. I propose that the illusory experience offered by such texts provides the individual with the opportunity to reorganize schemata without the fear of unpleasant practical or social consequence. ...

My claim is that the primary function of certain discourses is to effect a change in the schemata of their readers. Sensations of pleasure, escape, profundity, and elevation are conceivably offshoots of this function. So too is the high social esteem afforded to discourse with no other apparent social or practical function. ...

The category of schema-refreshing discourse, whose primary function is to effect change in schemata, will include many of those discourses described as 'literary'. This is not to say, however, that all literature is schema refreshing or that all schema-refreshing discourse is literature. The borders of the two types are not absolutely coterminous. (Nor, for that matter, are they precise.) Certainly, there are many discourses which are not generally accepted into the canon of literature, but whose primary value is the disruption of schemata.

▷ *'The boundaries here are fuzzy.' Which boundaries are fuzzy, and why?*

▷ *'... there are many discourses which are not generally accepted into the canon of literature, but whose primary value is the disruption of schemata.' Can you give examples of such discourses?*

Text 9

H.G. WIDDOWSON: *Practical Stylistics: An Approach to Poetry*. Oxford University Press 1992, pages 24–5

The author argues that, unlike other types of discourse, poetry is cut off from normal social practice. Its interpretation does not depend on being referred to some external situational context. So the poet must of necessity compensate for this lack of normal contextual connection by creating unique patterns of language within the context of the poem itself, thereby representing an elusive alternative to familiar social reality.

Poetry...in common with all art, necessarily challenges the adequacy of the established order. But this is not to replace it with a competing social orthodoxy, for with poetry there is no fixity. Rather it reveals that there is a reality which conventions cannot of their nature accommodate, in some dimension of meaning between the interstices of what is communal and familiar. For the socially sanctioned ways of using language to describe or expound or explain are not the only ways of using language. The meanings which are encoded to key in with the recurrent contexts of social life are not the only meanings which can be expressed. Once the demands of such contexts are suspended, other meanings, potential within the language, can be released and realigned. Representation, then, as a mode of meaning, is bound to be disruptive and to require a readiness to adopt different ways of reading and thinking for its realization. But in undermining the established and orthodox order of things, poetry sets up an alternative order of its own. For no matter how dispersed its propositional content might be in comparison with what is customary, it is held in place by the prosodic patterning of metre and rhyme. In denying one kind of regularity, the poem asserts its own.

I have argued, then, that the reading of a poem involves the realization of represented meaning. Since this meaning is unstable, elusive of its nature, held in precarious poise within the patterns of verse, it cannot be transposed into other terms, for this would be reduce it to reference, to the kind of conventional statement that it challenges. It follows, of course, that there can never be any definitive interpretation. ... All poems, and indeed all forms of art, contain within their very design the potential of multiple significance. It is precisely because they express realities which cannot be brought within the bounds of social convention that they are relevant. There are ideas and experience particular to the individual which cannot be made general within the scope of rational description or explanation. Poems represent them, fashion them into a form which we can apprehend without being able to explain.

▷ *The author argues that poetry represents types of possible experience which other normative and socially sanctioned discourses seek to suppress. In what respect does this argument conflict with the views expressed in Texts 6 and 7?*

▷ *Does this view of poetry imply that it typically belongs to the category of schema-refreshing discourse discussed in Text 8?*

Text 10
RONALD CARTER and WALTER NASH: *Seeing Through Language: A Guide to Styles of English Writing*. Blackwell 1990, pages 16–18

The authors argue that the notion of literary language as a clearly defined category should be replaced by one which sees literary language as a continuum, a cline of literariness in language use with some uses of language being marked as more literary than others.

…The term literariness is an important one in this book and is widely employed. There is space here only for a preliminary defining example of what we understand by this term. It can be most effectively explained by reference to the way language is used in the following advertisement:

You can't see through a Guinness

The advertisement is of course accompanied pictorially: in this case, this is a picture of a bar with two glasses of beer placed on the bar counter. The beers are of two different types—one is a light, lager-type beer, the other is Guinness beer which is a dark and opaque liquid. Through the transparent light beer we can see a distant game of cricket being played which those in the bar are all engaged in watching. In this context the caption *You can't see through a Guinness* acquires extra significance. In particular, a further semantic overlay accrues to the phrasal verb *see through*, which has two meanings in English: literally, to 'see through' is to look through something which is transparent and which does not impede vision; the second sense is that we 'see through' people or things which intend to deceive or which are deceptive or duplicitous. By extension, therefore, beer which is transparent can be seen through as not genuine. The *real* beer is therefore the Guinness beer. It is a beer we can trust.

Plays on words, semantic ambiguities—call them what we may—as well as figures of speech such as metaphor, or rhythmic patterning or allusiveness are generally regarded as belonging to a special and separate domain of literary language. The example of the Guinness advertisement demonstrates that this is not *exclusively* the case. Metaphor is an even more pervasive feature of language use, found in everyday conversations, articles and newspaper headlines such as:

Slums Are a Disease, Claims Minister

Rhythmic and phonological patterning occurs in many children's playground games while allusiveness is again a pervasive feature of advertisements. ... The main point to be underlined here is that features of language use more normally associated with literary contexts are found in what are conventionally thought of as non-literary contexts. It is for this reason that the term *literariness* is preferred to any term which suggests an absolute division between literary and non-literary. It is, in our view, more accurate to speak of degrees of literariness in language use.

▷ *Why, do you think, is 'literariness' not an absolute but a conditional phenomenon?*

▷ *How far do you think 'literariness' relates to the idea of 'schema refreshing discourse' discussed in Text 8?*

Chapter 4
Perspectives on meaning

Text 11
SHLOMITH RIMMON-KENAN: *Narrative Fiction:*
Contemporary Poetics. Methuen 1983, pages 71–3

'Point of view' is one of the most troublesome terms in literary
theory, all the more so because narratologists and critics have
been in the habit of using it in various ways. In an attempt to
clear up the consequent confusion, the author of the follow-
ing text introduces yet another term, namely 'focalization'.

The story is presented in the text through the mediation of some
'prism', 'perspective', 'angle of vision', verbalized by the narrator
though not necessarily his. Following Genette (1972) [*Narrative*
Discourse, Cornell University Press], I call this mediation 'focalization'. However, since Anglo-American readers are likely to
associate 'prism', 'perspective', or 'angle of vision' with the more
common term 'point of view', I shall begin by explaining why I
substitute 'focalization' for it.

Genette considers 'focalization' to have a degree of abstract-
ness which avoids the specifically visual connotations of 'point of
view'. ... It seems to me, however, that the term 'focalization' is
not free of optical-photographic connotations, and—like 'point
of view'—its purely visual sense has to be broadened to include
cognitive, emotive and ideological orientation. ... My own reason
for choosing 'focalization' is different from Genette's, although it
resides precisely in his treatment of it as a technical term.
Genette's treatment has the great advantage of dispelling the confusion between perspective and narration which often occurs
when 'point of view' or similar terms are used.

As Genette has shown, most studies of point of view...treat
two related but different questions as if they were interchangeable. Briefly formulated, these questions are 'who sees?' *v.* 'who
speaks?' Obviously, a person (and, by analogy, a narrative agent)
is capable of both speaking and seeing, and even of doing both
things at the same time—a state of affairs which facilitates the
confusion between the two activities. Moreover, it is almost impossible to speak without betraying some personal 'point of view', if

only through the very language used. But a person (and, by analogy, a narrative agent) is also capable of undertaking to tell what another person sees or has seen. Thus, speaking and seeing, narration and focalization, may, but need not, be attributed to the same agent. The distinction between the two activities is a theoretical necessity, and only on its basis can the interrelations between them be studied with precision. ...

...focalization and narration are separate in so-called first-person retrospective narratives, although this is usually ignored by studies of point of view. Pip, in Dickens's *Great Expectations*, narrates events that happened to him in the past:

'You are to wait here, you boy', said Estella and disappeared and closed the door.

I took the opportunity of being alone in the court-yard, to look at my coarse hands and my common boots. My opinion of those accessories was not favourable. They had never troubled me before, but they troubled me now, as vulgar appendages.
(1978, pp. 91–2 [Penguin]. Orig. Publ. 1860/61)

Although, this is a record of things as the child saw, felt, understood them, words like 'accessories' and 'appendages' are clearly not within a child's vocabulary. The narrator is Pip, the adult, while the focalizer is Pip, the child.

▷ *What is the relationship between 'focalizer' and 'narrator' in the opening passage from Ishiguro's novel* An Artist of the Floating World, *discussed in Section 1, Chapter 4?*

Text 12
MICHAEL TOOLAN: *Narrative: A Critical Linguistic Introduction* (2nd edn.) Routledge 2001, page 79

Conventionally, first-person narrators who are also characters in the fictional world are taken to be reliable informants. But this is not always so: first-person narrators often turn out to be uninformed, insincere, or even untruthful. The following text discusses what happens when readers are confronted with such narrators.

...[we may begin to consider] what happens when a narrator wilfully or unwittingly distorts, misleads, or suppresses. The topic of narrational unreliability is an extremely rich theme, and has been probed by critics and theorists extensively for a very long time (cf. Lawrence's warning: 'Never trust the teller, trust the tale'), especially vigorously in the last forty years, since Booth's *Rhetoric of Fiction* appeared. Of particular concern is the (un)reliability of intradiegetic narrators, i.e. narrators visible—if only by way of the first-person pronoun—within the narrative. That is to say, the detection of 'corrupt' narration is especially commonly a challenge set for readers by intrusive/evaluative first-person narrators. ... Narratorial unreliability in modern fiction is very widespread, ...

We attribute unreliability to any narrator the veracity of whose account we come to suspect. Some narrators are liars, or consciously flatter themselves and are clearly intended to be seen as attempting to deceive; other narrators mislead for less culpable reasons: e.g. they may have the limited knowledge of a young narrator, or be learning disabled like Benjy in *The Sound and the Fury*. Personal involvement with events—especially when the narrator is a direct or indirect victim of those events—may often give rise to narratorial suppression, distortion, prevarication, and so on. ... In a more general way, abnormal values may give rise to a type of unreliability that makes it difficult to decide whether we have a normal narrator telling terrible things with much covert irony, or simply an awful narrator. In assessing veracity and reliability, we have to act rather like a juror, weighing the evidence, looking for internal contradictions in what a narrator says (especially when they serve that narrator's purposes) or a clash between a narrator's representations of things and those of (other) characters whom we have independent grounds for trusting and respecting. The great attraction and danger of unreliable narration is...that no clear moral or ideological stance is spelt out and held to, and we as readers are not *told* what to think. But a fully articulated theory of what unreliability consists in, and of the grounds for attributing it to one narrator but not another, remains elusive and contentious.

▷ *Why should narrator unreliability be such an extremely rich theme? In other words, what is the great attraction to the reader?*

▷ *Would you agree that unreliable narration is to a large extent a matter of the rhetorical structure of the novel and that, therefore, a study of its style may be very helpful? Or is it more than just a 'verbal' matter?*

▷ *Can you point out some features in the opening passage of Ishiguro's* An Artist of the Floating World *(Section 1, Chapter 4) which seriously undermine the account of the first-person narrator?*

Text 13

JEREMY HAWTHORN: *Studying the Novel: An Introduction* (3rd edn.) Arnold 1997, pages 104–5

This text suggests that turning novels into plays or films might be conducive to a better understanding of the narrative technique of the novel itself.

One term which has, I think, a useful summarizing scope here is *narrative situation*. We can indicate what this term covers by asking about the relationship *between the telling and what is told*. Is the narrator personified, if so is he/she a character involved in the action of the work, is the narrative dramatic or immediate or distanced? — and so on. Narrative situation thus includes both perspective and voice, ...

Sometimes attempts to turn novels into plays or films have the effect of demonstrating how crucial their particular narrative situation is. Joseph Conrad attempted dramatizations of a number of his works, all of which were more or less disastrous. I think we can easily understand that a dramatization of *The Secret Agent* (which Conrad actually completed) *would* be disastrous because it necessarily loses what is at the heart of the work's power: the bitter but pityingly ironic attitude of the narrator towards the characters and events of the novel. ...

When a novel is dramatized we ... have the shaping hand of a director, and the interpretations of the individual actors. But the novel itself gives both far less and far more: the novelist guides our attention to some things and prevents us from becoming concerned with others .... . Much is thus 'cut out'. But what is left is suggestive and artistically rich, such that although a film of a scene from a novel may seem to include much more concrete detail than the novel, it is often more difficult artistically to organize this detail compared to the original arrangement on the printed page. Thus our experience of the film of a novel is often that it seems flatter, less complex, than a reading of the novel itself.

▷ *How far do the concepts of 'perspective' and 'voice' correspond with those of 'focalization' and 'narration' in Text 11? How, for instance, would the role of the omniscient narrator be accounted for in these terms?*

▷ *Which aspect(s) of the narrative situation in the opening passage from Ishiguro's* An Artist of the Floating World *(Section 1, Chapter 4) might be lost in a film adaptation? For instance, does the role of the narrator pose a problem for a film director?*

▷ *'...our experience of the film of a novel is often that it seems flatter, less complex, than a reading of the novel itself'. Is this true of your own experience?*

Chapter 5
The language of literary representation

Text 14
GEOFFREY N. LEECH and MICHAEL H. SHORT: *Style in Fiction: A Linguistic Introduction to English Fictional Prose.* Longman 1981, pages 325–6

This text discusses the stylistic features of Free Indirect Speech (FIS), as distinct from Indirect Speech (IS), and what effects they have on the nature of the narrative.

FIS usually occurs in the context of sentences of narrative report, and, given the preponderance of the third-person narrator telling his tale in the past tense, its characteristic features in the novel are almost always the presence of third-person pronouns and past tense, which correspond with the form of narrative report and indicate indirectness, along with a number of features both positive and negative indicating freeness. Thus it is, as it were, a free form 'purporting' to be IS. A good example is the portrayal of the lawyer Mr Shepherd's speech in [Jane Austen's] *Persuasion*:

'Then I take it for granted,' observed Sir Walter, 'that his face is about as orange as the cuffs and capes of my livery.'

Mr Shepherd hastened to assure him, that Admiral Croft was a very hale, hearty, well-looking man, a little weather-beaten, to be sure, but not much; and quite the gentleman in all his notions and behaviour;—not likely to make the smallest difficulty about terms;—only wanted a comfortable home, and to get into it as soon as possible;—knew he must pay for his convenience;—knew what rent a ready-furnished house of that consequence might fetch;—should not have been surprised if Sir Walter had asked more;—had inquired about the manor;—would be glad of the deputation, certainly, but made no great point of it;—said he sometimes took out a gun, but never killed;—quite the gentleman. [Ch. 3]

Sir Walter's speech is in the direct form, appropriate for the speech of a man totally sure of himself. Mr Shepherd's role, however, is that of the deferential functionary, and so Jane Austen uses the more self-effacing indirect form for him. He begins in IS which then blends into FIS mainly by virtue of the fact that the subordinating conjunction *that* and the subject are not repeated. These negative syntactic indications are reinforced by colloquial lexical forms, especially the fussy lawyer's reiteration of the reassuring phrase 'quite the gentleman', and the dashes, which indicate that we are only getting snatches of the conversation. Thus we are presented with a form which has indications of an intervening narrator but also some flavour of the original speech. The chopping of the speech brings out the parallels in form of the statements about the admiral, as if to underline the inexhaustibility of the lawyer's store of eager reassurances. All these factors help to put an ironic distance between the reader and Mr Shepherd, allowing room for us to feel that his persuasiveness is for his own benefit rather than Sir Walter's. This ability to give the flavour of the character's words but also to keep the narrator in an intervening position between character and reader makes FIS an extremely useful vehicle for casting an ironic light on what the character says.

▷ *How do the points made here about FIS relate to what is said in Text 12 about narrator unreliability?*

▷ Why should FIS be 'an extremely useful vehicle for casting an ironic light on what the character says'?

Text 15

KATIE WALES: *The Language of James Joyce.* Macmillan 1992, pages 77–8

The author shows that James Joyce's Ulysses, *which is pre-eminently known as a 'stream-of-consciousness' novel, is in fact a work which contains a plurality of perspectives and representations of speech and thought.*

In *Ulysses* the perspective is dramatically shifted in the fourth episode ('Calypso'), and the reader is confronted...by a new centre of focalisation, a new 'hero'. The novel begins anew, in effect, since it is breakfast time again, this time for Leopold Bloom:

Mr Leopold Bloom ate with relish the inner organs of beasts and fowls. He liked thick giblet soup, nutty gizzards, a stuffed roast heart, liver slices fried with crustcrumbs, fried hencods' roes. Most of all he liked grilled mutton kidneys which gave to his palate a fine tang of faintly scented urine.

Kidneys were in his mind as he moved about the kitchen softly, righting her breakfast things on the humpy tray. Gelid light and air were in the kitchen but out of doors gentle summer morning everywhere. Made him feel a bit peckish.

The coals were reddening.

Another slice of bread and butter: three, four: right. She didn't like her plate full. Right. ... (4.1–12)

The reader...is thrust *in medias res* (Who is *her* and *she*?), and very quickly now into the workings of Bloom's mind, via a shift in perspective and idiosyncrasies of narrative. The use of situational deictic words like *her* and *the* [humpy tray] suggest a familiar scene, familiar to the character; 'Made him feel a bit peckish' is in third-person narration, but we can note the ellipsis of subject and the colloquial 'a bit peckish': free indirect thought perhaps (cp. 'Makes me feel a bit peckish'), although Bloom probably never consciously makes the causal connection between the weather and his appetite ('Made him...'). 'The coals were reddening' could be either a descriptive piece of narration, or Bloom's observation.

Interior monologue appears to start with 'Another slice of bread and butter': but the past tense 'She *didn't*' suggests free indirect thought again, followed by free direct thought ('Right'.)

This then, is the common pattern of Joyce's representation of the inner voices of his main characters: interior monologue is subtly interwoven with narrative and indirect thought with the focalisation or point of view predominantly that of the character. ...the result is often a complex and ambiguous 'dialogic' style, with subtle shifts often within one and the same sentence.

▷ *How far do you think this text illustrates the points made about narration and focalization in Text 11?*

▷ *This text focuses attention on Free Indirect Thought (FIT). How do you think this relates to what is said about Free Indirect Speech (FIS) in Text 14?*

Chapter 6
Perspectives on literary interpretation

Text 16
MICK SHORT: 'Literature and Language' in M. Coyle, P. Garside, M. Kelsall, and J. Peck (eds.): *Encyclopedia of Literature and Criticism*. Routledge 1990, pages 1084–5

The author here addresses some problematic aspects of the role that 'evaluation' and 'interpretation' play in literary criticism and stylistics, suggesting that the two are interdependent, and ultimately founded on linguistic analysis and description.

...I believe that two of the most important academic questions to be addressed in the study of literature are why and how particular meanings and effects are present in particular literary works. And I cannot see how such questions can be answered without recourse to detailed linguistic analysis. The 'how' and the 'why' are important because:

1 as critics we are duty bound to give detailed support for our interpretative conclusions;

2 we need a way of checking whether the understandings we intuitively arrive at are reasonable, and careful stylistic analysis provides a large part of what is required for such a check;

3 if we are faced with someone who does not see our interpretation or who disagrees with it, we need some way, other than merely 'pointing', to help demonstrate that meaning or effect.

I do *not* believe, by any means, that this linguistic-critical activity is the only one critics should be engaged in. Far from it. But I do believe that the detailed answering of 'why?' and 'how?' cannot be ignored by critics and that recourse to careful linguistic description linked to interpretation provides much (but not all) of what is required.

The point may be made clearer by a diagram showing what I would consider to be the essential core of critical activity:

Evaluation

↑

Interpretation

↑

Description of textual structure

Critics usually say that the prime objective of their enterprise is the evaluation of literary works. This evaluative activity presupposes interpretation, as it makes no sense to say how good a text is unless one understands it. In criticism, intuitive understanding has to be made explicit in the form of an interpretation. However, textual interpretation itself presupposes reaction to the structure of the text. This structure turns out to be largely, but not entirely (cf. plot), linguistic, ... In spite of the fact that evaluation is the goal of criticism, most of the effort in twentieth-century literary studies has been directed at interpretative matters. Stylistics has a slightly different focus in that it is centrally interested in making explicit the detailed relationship between textual structure and interpretation, and how the reader gets from the former to the latter. If criticism is to be a well-founded discipline, this explicit demonstration of the grounds for interpretation is as important as the need to state clearly the interpretations themselves.

▷ *Do you think 'description' and 'interpretation' are distinct activities, as this author proposes?*

▷ '...*careful linguistic description linked to interpretation pro-*
vides much (but not all) of what is required'. How far do you
think this statement is borne out by the discussion of Heaney's
poem in Section 1, Chapter 6?

Texts 17 and 18

Texts 17 and 18 present different treatments of this poem by
Philip Larkin, Text 17 from a literary-critical and Text 18
from a stylistic-analytical perspective.

The Trees

The trees are coming into leaf
Like something almost being said;
The recent buds relax and spread,
Their greenness is a kind of grief.

Is it that they are born again
And we grow old? No, they die too.
Their yearly trick of looking new
Is written down in rings of grain.

Yet still the unresting castles thresh
In fullgrown thickness every May.
Last year is dead, they seem to say,
Begin afresh, afresh, afresh.

(Philip Larkin. *Collected Poems*, page 166)

Text 17
ANDREW MOTION: 'Philip Larkin and Symbolism' in
Stephan Regan (ed.): *Philip Larkin*. Macmillan New
Casebooks 1997, pages 34–5

In 'Church Going' and 'The Building', as in 'The Explosion',
Larkin looks to familiar social and natural rituals for the inspiration that might formerly have come from the church. In other
poems he concentrates on the rewards of the natural world more
exclusively—but, as 'Cut Grass' or 'Forget What Did' illustrate,
they provide an equivalently ambiguous comfort. 'The Trees' is
another example. ... 'The Trees' denies that nature allows people

to believe in their immortality. But, while this denial provokes the same vulnerability as that produced by lack of faith in orthodox religion, there are positive aspects as well. In spite of their steadily increasing age, the trees do at least 'seem' to return unchanged each year, and invite the speaker to follow their example and begin his life 'afresh'. Their towering solidity (they are like 'castles') dwarfs his knowledge of mortality. And this is their consolation: their rejuvenation confirms his human potential, without deceiving him into thinking that it can last for ever. Larkin, here as elsewhere, sees through appearances at the same time as he seizes on them.

That said, he is much less interested in nature for its own sake than for the opportunities it offers to moralise about the human condition. It is this which accounts for what Donald Davie has uncharitably called 'his imperiousness towards the non-human'; it is in fact not imperiousness but an admission that the natural world is beautiful, restorative and necessary, yet also vulnerable and transient.

Text 18

PETER VERDONK: 'The liberation of the icon: A brief survey from classical rhetoric to cognitive stylistics' in *Journal of Literary Studies* Vol. 15, Numbers 3/4, 1999, pages 299–300

The very first word in the title is the definite article 'the'. Evidently, it does not refer to trees mentioned earlier in the discourse or something unique which is common knowledge and therefore already shared by speaker and listener, like 'The sun sets in the west'. All the same, informed readers will not be surprised because in literary discourses the definite article is quite often the very first word. The rhetorical effect is that readers get the feeling that they share their knowledge schema, which has thus been activated, with that of the narrator or, as in this case, with that of the poet's persona. As a result readers are drawn as it were into the discourse, they feel a degree of involvement, and they are therefore encouraged to further explore not only their prestructured knowledge of 'trees' but also to call up any other related cognitive structures. Besides, it produces in readers the sensation that the poet's persona wants his experience and emotions to be absorbed into the reader's world. Interestingly, this deictic function of the definite article appears to provide evidence that readers do make use of cognitive schemata in their interpretation of discourses.

The first line 'The trees are coming into leaf' is likely to confirm the reader's corresponding schema about the beginning of a yearly repeated event in nature. However, knowing the discourse genre of poetry, the reader may be expected to transform these bare facts into a metaphorical message for humankind, particularly because this message is suggested, though not explicitly expressed, in the second line 'Like something almost being said'. Clearly, this line necessitates an adjustment or even a complete revision of the reader's schema about THE GROWTH OF TREES, for trees coming into leaf are not supposed to be able to speak. It is only natural, though, that readers still want to know the message of the trees, and searching through their mental knowledge stores, and perhaps simultaneously renewing them, they are likely to produce their own version of the content of the message.

In the third and fourth lines we find the same discursive process as in the first two lines. The third line 'The recent buds relax and spread' confirms the reader's existing schema of a particular natural phenomenon, though the verb 'relax' in this context seems deviant or foregrounded and may well lead to a slight adjustment of the relevant schema. However, the fourth line 'Their greenness is a kind of grief' requires a drastic revision of the reader's experiential knowledge and therewith presents a challenge to metaphorization. At this point the reader may tentatively infer that the silent message of the trees is an annually repeated reminder of the fact that this ritual of nature implies a paradox. For, on the one hand, there is the promise of new life and continuity as expressed in the phrase 'their greenness', and on the other hand, there is the sense of finiteness and mortality, which is alluded to in the qualified phrase 'a kind of grief'. Since according to cognitive linguists, metaphors are the foundation of the human conceptual system, many readers may well feel inclined to relate this disquieting paradox to the human condition, in particular to the cycle of birth and death.

…Now it only remains for me to draw your attention to an interesting meeting point between schema theory and the ideas on foregrounding and parallelism originating from formalist literary theories. Foregrounding and parallelism were seen as the essence of poetry, but at the time that formalism was fashionable, they were never related to the active role of the reader in the negotiation of meaning. ... Recent publications...have pointed out that schema theory might fill this void, by hypothesising that notably through the foregrounded or unorthodox formal aspects of poetry the cognitive schemata of readers are activated, inter-connected and completely or partially revised.

▷ *Point out which elements in the two approaches support the view expressed in Section 1, Chapter 6 that the relationship between literary criticism and stylistics may be regarded as complementary.*

▷ *Refer back to Text 8 and identify some foregrounded textual features in Larkin's poem that may be said to 'refresh' your cognitive schemata.*

Chapter 7
Stylistics and ideological perspectives

Text 19
SARA MILLS: *Feminist Stylistics*. Routledge 1995, page 185

Feminist stylistics aims to provide readers with analytic and critical tools to identify and resist gender bias in texts. This is not always easy because such bias may often take the guise of common sense. In this text, Mills makes use of the concept of 'focalization' (see Text 11) to show the gender bias of a sup-posedly neutral narration.

...there are signals in texts as to the centre of focalization, and this does not necessarily coincide with the narrative voice, although it may. Neither is the focalizer [the one who sees] necessarily static, but may shift from one internal character to another, or to an external narrator. The importance of the concept of focaliza-tion is that it slants the emotive and ideological content of a text, and represents the experience of the protagonists partially. Below [is an example] of how a feminist analysis of texts could utilize focalization.

...consider the following passage from *A Woman of Substance*:

> Paul finally took her to him with flaring passion, his ardour gentled but in no way muted by his tenderness. Silken arms and legs entwined him, fluid and weightless, yet they pulled him down...down...down.
>
> (Taylor Bradford 1981: 667)

The narrative voice is external and omniscient. It is not present in the text as a fictional character but is external, yet can reveal the characters' motivations and thoughts to the readers. So, theoretically, the narrative is reported by a disembodied, impersonal voice which can record objectively the course of events and the psychology of the characters. However, the 'vision' [i.e. the focalization] is Paul's: it is his experience of the event which is narrated. The woman Emma is presented not as her own consciousness, but as Paul experiences her—as disembodied limbs, 'silken arms and legs', without weight or form, 'fluid and weightless'. A further linguistic signal that it is Paul's consciousness from which the event is focalized is that the pronouns 'him' and 'his' suggest a subject which has unity of mind and body. For Emma, however, the pronoun 'her' is replaced by 'they', referring to her limbs. By this linguistic device, her body has been separated from her consciousness: her body is present as focalized by Paul. Her unified consciousness is not available to the reader. The focalizing of the scene through the male's experience inevitably represents the female as the object of the male gaze. Mediating her textual representation by the male's perception of her subordinates her sexual pleasure to his, or means that hers may be created as a result of his. Furthermore, whilst the text seems to be narrated by an external narrator, there are points where the narrative voice and Paul's consciousness seem to merge even more fully. For example, through the use of free indirect speech [i.e. FID], Paul's thoughts are not represented as such, but his thoughts and the narrator's seem to become the same as, for example, in 'down ... down ... down' where the sensations of Paul are described by the narrator in words which could be Paul's own thoughts. Where this happens, the focalization seems to be at one and the same time that of an internal character and that of an external narrator.

▷ *Could you rewrite the passage from* A Woman of Substance *in such a way that the centre of focalization shifts from Paul to Emma? What does your attempt tell you about the general effect of focalization?*

Text 20

NORMAN FAIRCLOUGH: 'Dialogue in the public sphere' in Srikant Sarangi and Malcolm Coulthard (eds.): *Discourse and Social Life*. Pearson Education 2000, pages 176–7

The author here identifies a specific linguistic feature, the pronoun 'we', as being of particular ideological significance in the political text he analyses.

Inclusive 'we' as a device for avoiding division leads in some cases to incoherence. The following extract from [a] speech [by Tony Blair to the Confederation of British Industry in 1998] is a case in point:

> Private sector income growth gives serious cause for concern. It would be the worst of short-termism now to pay ourselves more today at the cost of higher interest rates, fewer jobs.... It is really up to us: the greater the responsibility, the bigger the reward. We have learnt that lesson so often in the past. We cannot afford to learn it again.

Who is the 'we' here? It is an inclusive 'we', yet it is clearly not the British people as a whole who are 'paying themselves more'. The reference is specifically to the private sector. One division which 'we' covers over here is between private sector and public sector—the income gap between people who work in the private sector and people who work in the public sector is growing under New Labour. But there is also another division which 'we' covers over, though it is hinted at in the wording 'pay ourselves'. It is only really those in senior management who control pay who 'pay themselves'. The other division is between senior managers and the rest—that income gap is also growing under New Labour. But Blair is after all addressing the Confederation of British Industry, i.e. senior managers; they will no doubt pick up the hint without Blair needing to foreground the division for his wider audience. So, we might say that the inclusive language in this case causes obfuscation, it covers over social relations and divisions—except that the incoherence of 'pay ourselves more' leaves a trace of this obfuscation. It is not a trace which someone listening to the speech, or listening to or reading reports about it, will necessarily notice, but it is the sort of trace which some people will notice (maybe those whose pay is decreasing or not increasing, as well as Blair's audience in the CBI), and which may become more widely noticeable and noticed in a changing political climate. Of course, the contrast between the inclusive discourse and the exclusive club Blair is addressing on the occasion enhances its noticeability! What I am suggesting then is that an inclusive political discourse is difficult to sustain without incoherences, and that those incoherences may, in certain circumstances, expose it to risk.

▷ *How far do you think these inferences about the wider sociopolitical significance of the use of this pronoun 'we' are warranted?*

▷ *This is a stylistic analysis of a non literary text. How, in your view, and with reference to examples from Section 1, is it different from the stylistic analysis of a literary text?*

References

The references which follow can be classified into introductory level (marked ■□□), more advanced and consequently more technical (marked ■■□), and specialized, very demanding (marked ■■■).

Chapter 1
The concept of style

■□□

RONALD CARTER and WALTER NASH: *Seeing Through Language: A Guide to Styles of English Writing*. Blackwell 1990 (*see* Text 10)

This book fulfils the promise of its designedly ambiguous title by developing the reader's awareness of the use of language both as a tool of perception and as an instrument of duplicity.

■□□

ELIZABETH CLOSS TRAUGOTT and MARY LOUISE PRATT: *Linguistics for Students of Literature*. Harcourt Brace Jovanovich 1980 (*see* Text 3)

This useful book contains some readable chapters on definitions of style and the application of linguistics to literary phenomena.

■■□

PETER VERDONK: 'The liberation of the icon: A brief survey from classical rhetoric to cognitive stylistics' in *Journal of Literary Studies/Tydskrif vir Literatuurwetenskap* 15/3–4, 1999 (*see* Text 18)

This article provides a general perspective on the historical development of stylistics as a discipline and on current emphases within this field.

■■■

JEAN JACQUES WEBER: *The Stylistics Reader: From Roman Jakobson to the Present.* Arnold 1996

This informative book brings together key essays and writings which mark the development of stylistics as a discipline from its formalist beginnings to the contextualized, discourse-based approaches practised nowadays.

Chapters 2 and 3
Style in literature: Text and discourse

■■□

RONALD CARTER and PAUL SIMPSON (eds.): *Language, Discourse and Literature: An Introductory Reader in Discourse Stylistics.* Unwin Hyman 1989 (*see* Text 7)

This collection of essays demonstrates the use of discourse analysis as a stylistic tool. Interestingly, the contributors employ the term discourse in both its pragmatic and its ideological senses (*See* Glossary).

■■□

GUY COOK: *Discourse and Literature: The Interplay of Form and Mind.* Oxford University Press 1994 (*see* Text 8)

A stimulating book which argues that literariness arises when the linguistic make-up of texts challenges the reader's established structures of reality, or schemata, and causes schema refreshment.

■■□
ROGER FOWLER: *Literature as Social Discourse: The Practice of Linguistic Criticism*. Batsford Academic and Educational Ltd 1981 (*see* Text 6)

The recurrent theme in this collection of essays is that literature is a kind of social discourse and, like any other form of discourse, reflects and influences relations within society.

■□□
H. G. WIDDOWSON: *Practical Stylistics: An Approach to Poetry*. Oxford University Press 1992 (*see* Text 9)

The central theme of this invaluable book is the rejection of the current trend to treat literature as social discourse. Instead it focuses on how the language of poetry empowers the reader to think up realities other than those which are socially sanctioned. A detailed Notes section comments insightfully on issues such as linguistic determinism, the socialization of literature, literature as text and discourse, and intertextuality.

■□□
MICK SHORT: *Exploring the Language of Poems, Plays and Prose*. Addison Wesley Longman 1996

This is a highly accessible and systematic introduction to stylistics. Through detailed analyses followed by challenging exercises, the author discusses how meanings and effects are created in poetry, drama, and fiction.

■□□
PAUL SIMPSON: *Language through Literature: An Introduction*. Routledge 1997

An entertaining introduction to key topics in English language study through the use of examples from poetry, prose, and drama. Chapter 1 describes stylistics as a method of applied linguistics using textual analysis to explore the structure and function of language.

Chapter 4
Perspectives on meaning

■■□

SHLOMITH RIMMON-KENAN: *Narrative Fiction: Contemporary Poetics*. Methuen 1983 (*see* Text 11)

This is an influential book on fictional narratives organized around the aspects involved in their construction: events, characters, time, characterization, focalization, narration, and the text and its reading.

■■□

MICHAEL TOOLAN: *Narrative: A Critical Linguistic Introduction* (2nd edn.) Routledge 2001 (*see* Text 12)

This is the second edition of an authoritative introduction to narratology and linguistic approaches to narrative structure. A wide range of topics includes plot structure, time manipulation, point of view, film, children's narrative, and newspaper stories.

Chapter 5
The language of literary representation

■■□

GEOFFREY N. LEECH and MICHAEL H. SHORT: *Style in Fiction: A Linguistic Introduction to English Fictional Prose*. Longman 1981 (*see* Text 14)

A classic book which has had a profound influence on the study of style in prose fiction. In particular Chapter 10 on speech and thought presentation has initiated numerous studies of the topic.

■□□

MICHAEL TOOLAN: *Language in Literature: An Introduction to Stylistics*. Arnold 1998

This book provides an activity-based introduction to stylistics. Chapter 5 discusses engagingly the representation of character speech and thought in literary texts, while Chapter 6 is an equally lively account of the structure of narratives.

Chapter 6
Perspectives on literary interpretation

■■☐

RICHARD BRADFORD: *Stylistics*, in the series 'The New Critical Idiom'. Routledge 1997

This book discusses the role of stylistics in twentieth-century criticism and the evolution of literary style since the Renaissance, and follows the development of stylistics from classical rhetoric to post-structuralism. It also considers the relationships between style and gender, and between style and evaluative judgement.

■■■

M. COYLE, P. GARSIDE, M. KELSALL, and J. PECK (eds.): *Encyclopedia of Literature and Criticism*. Routledge 1990 (see Text 16)

Linguistic students crossing the stylistic bridge to literature may well benefit from this encyclopedia, which is in fact a collection of some ninety essays on a wide variety of topics related to literary theories, genres, schools of criticism, production and reception, and contexts.

■☐☐

JOANNA THORNBORROW and SHÂN WAREING: *Patterns in Language: An Introduction to Language and Literary Style*. Routledge 1998

This is a user-friendly guide to stylistics with a strong focus on the recurrence of language patterns used by writers. Chapter 6 relates stylistics to other literary perspectives by considering the stylistic characteristics of realist, modernist, and postmodernist texts.

Chapter 7
Stylistics and ideological perspectives

■□□

ROGER FOWLER: *Language in the News: Discourse and Ideology in the Press*. Routledge 1991

Taking the perspective of a critical linguist, the author discloses in a lucid style the ideologies at work in the language of newspapers, considering their representations of gender, power, and law and order.

■□□

SARA MILLS: *Feminist Stylistics*. Routledge 1995 (*see* Text 19)

This well-written book aims to provide stylistic tools to expose gender bias in literary and non-literary texts. A useful feature of the book is the extensive list of questions which can be addressed to a text from a feminist perspective.

■□□

WALTER NASH: *Language in Popular Fiction*. Routledge 1990

In a witty style the author presents a stylistic analysis of popular fiction on three levels of investigation: verbal choice, narrative structure, and a level at which stylistic options are related to the ideologies of manliness and womanliness which readers bring to or derive from this genre.

■□□

SRIKANT SARANGI and MALCOLM COULTHARD (eds.): *Discourse and Social Life*. Pearson Education 2000 (*see* Text 20)

This is a collection of original papers by some of the best-known contemporary writers on discourse analysis and stylistics.

Collections of examples of stylistic analyses

All four examples provide instructive examples of stylistic analyses of a wide range of texts. All four also contain suggestions for further work.

■□□
RONALD CARTER (ed.): *Language and Literature: An Introductory Reader in Stylistics*. Allen & Unwin 1982

■□□
J. CULPEPER, M. SHORT, and P. VERDONK (eds.): *Exploring the Language of Drama: From Text to Context*. Routledge 1998

■□□
PETER VERDONK (ed.): *Twentieth-century Poetry: From Text to Context*. Routledge 1993

■□□
PETER VERDONK and JEAN JACQUES WEBER (eds.): *Twentieth-century Fiction: From Text to Context*. Routledge 1995

Reference works

In addition to the books cited above, the following reference works can be consulted for information on specific literary-critical, linguistic, and stylistic terms and concepts:

■■□
T. V. F. BROGAN (ed.): *The New Princeton Handbook of Poetic Terms*. Princeton University Press 1994

This is a very useful and readable reference book containing detailed discussions of poetic terms, and of topics such as intertextuality, linguistics and poetics, and rhetoric and style.

■■□

KATIE WALES: *A Dictionary of Stylistics* (2nd edn.) Pearson
Education 2001 (*see* Text 5)

This is an indispensable guide for any course in stylistics. It explains
clearly and concisely over 600 terms and concepts from literature, linguistics, rhetoric, and stylistics.

SECTION 4
Glossary

Page references to Section 1, Survey, are given at the end of each entry.

context Linguistic context refers to the surrounding features of language inside a **text**, while non-linguistic context includes any number of text-external features influencing the language and style of a text. [6, 19]

critical discourse analysis (CDA) A branch of linguistics which aims to reveal the implicit ideological forces at work in spoken or written texts. *See also* Text 20. [75]

deictics Textual cues such as *here*, *there*, *now*, *then*, *I*, and *you*, which locate a **discourse** in relation to the speaker's or writer's **perspective** or **point of view**, whether in space, time, or interpersonal relations. *See also* **place deictics, time deictics, person deictics.** [35]

deixis The process of contextual orientation (from the Greek word for 'pointing' or 'showing'). *See* **deictics.** [35]

direct speech (DS) A style of speech representation used when a narrator delegates **perspective** to the characters and leaves them to speak for themselves, e.g. *'It's frightfully dreary,' she said*: cf. **indirect speech (IS).** [23, 46]

direct thought (DT) A style of thought representation, which presupposes a privileged omniscience on the part of the narrator, e.g. *'It's frightfully dreary,' she thought*: cf. **indirect thought (IT).** [46]

discourse (1) The process of activation of a **text** by relating it to an appropriate **context**, in other words, the reader's or listener's reconstruction of the writer's or speaker's intended message. (2) An ideological construct of particular sociopolitical or cultural values. *See also* **ideology,** and Texts 5–9. [18, 75]

dominant reading The reading of a text that appears to be the most obvious and natural one because it is upheld by the dominant **ideologies** about the role of women in the society of the time. *See also* **feminist stylistics, resistant reading.** [70]

ellipsis The omission of one or more words from a **text,** which the hearer or reader can recover or guess from the **context** (from the Greek word for 'defective'). [4]

feminist stylistics A branch of stylistics which aims to provide readers with analytic and critical tools to identify and resist gender bias in texts. *See also* Text 19. [70]

figure The elements in a text which catch our attention (The brain sorts out information obtained though visual perception into two categories, which psychologists call figure and **ground.**) [44]

foregrounding The bringing of particular textual features into prominence, e.g. distinct patterns or parallelism, repetitions, and deviations from general linguistic rules or from the style expected in a specific **text type** or **genre,** or **context.** [6]

free indirect discourse (FID) This is an umbrella term for **free indirect speech (FIS)** and **free indirect thought (FIT).** FID has certain elements in common with both **direct speech (DS)** or **direct thought (DT),** e.g. *Charlotte concluded, 'I have to do it right now'* and **indirect speech (IS)** or **indirect thought (IT),** e.g. *Charlotte concluded that she had to do it right then.* For example, in the narrative sequence *Charlotte came to a firm decision. She had to do it right now,* the second sentence is in FID, combining the narrator perspective (third person and past tense: *She had to do it*) with the character perspective (**deictic** phrase: *right now*). *See also* Texts 14, 15. [48]

free indirect speech (FIS) *See* **free indirect discourse (FID).** [48]

free indirect thought (FIT) *See* **free indirect discourse (FID).** [48]

genre A culturally specific **text type,** e.g. newspaper article, blurb, novel, poem. [4, 11, 63]

given information Information which the speaker or writer assumes to be already known to the listener or reader: cf. **new information**. [37]

ground The elements in a text which serve as general contextual background. (The brain sorts out information obtained though visual perception into two categories, which psychologists call **figure** and ground.) [44]

ideological perspective The speaker or writer's **point of view** with respect to his or her sociopolitical beliefs and values. [38, 75]

ideology A set of social, cultural, and political beliefs and values which inform the way we think things ought to be. *See also* Text 20. [71]

indirect speech (IS) A style of speech representation in which the narrator reports only the content of what the character has said, but not its exact wording, e.g. an IS version of the **direct speech (DS)** *'It's frightfully dreary,' she said* is *She said that it was very dreary*: cf. **direct speech**. [47]

indirect thought (IT) A style of thought representation that presupposes even more interference by the narrator than in **indirect speech (IS)**. The linguistic structure is the same as it is for IS: e.g. an IT version of the **direct thought (DT)** *'It's frightfully dreary,' she thought* is *She thought that it was very dreary*: cf. **direct thought**. [47]

interior monologue *See* **stream of consciousness technique**. [51]

internal foregrounding A deviation from a linguistic pattern set up by the **text** itself, or a sudden change in the dominant style of a text: cf. **foregrounding**. [15]

intertextuality An echo of, or an allusion to, another **text**. [5, 62]

linguistic criticism The critical study of **discourse**, which assumes that the meaning of all **texts**, including literary ones, can be inferred from the social, institutional, and ideological conditions of their production and reception. *See also* Texts 6 and 9. [74]

modality Textual elements such as modal auxiliaries (e.g. *may, could, would*) and **sentence adverbs** (e.g. *perhaps, certainly*) signalling attitude and enabling speakers to express degrees of commitment to the truth or validity of what they are talking about, and to mitigate the effect of their words on the people they are talking to: cf. **ideological perspective**. [39]

new information Information which the speaker or writer assumes that the listener or reader cannot have acquired knowledge about from the **context**: cf. **given information**. [37]

person deictics Textual elements such as the first-person pronoun *I* (and its related forms *me, my, mine*) and the second-person pronoun *you* (and its related forms *your, yours*): cf. **place deictics, time deictics**. [35]

perspective In a literal sense, the physical angle of vision from which a story gets told, i.e. the narrator's spatial and temporal perspective. Metaphorically, it also implies the speaker's mental, emotional, and **ideological perspective**. *See also* **deictics**, and Texts 11, 13. [29]

place deictics Textual elements such as *here, there, behind, to the left* which refer the listener or reader to the situational **point of view** of the speaker or writer in the **discourse**: cf. **person deictics, time deictics**. [35]

point of view *See* **perspective**. [29]

pragmatics The study of what people mean by language when they use it in an appropriate **context** to achieve particular purposes: cf. **semantics**. [19]

reference The use of language to identify things in **context**: cf. **representation**. *See also* Text 9. [12, 74]

representation The use of language to create a **context** of reality rather than to identify aspects of an existing one; the projection through language of an alternative world: cf. **reference**. *See also* Text 9. [12, 34, 74]

resistant reading The process of deliberately denying the most obvious interpretation of a **text** and constructing an alternative one: cf. **dominant reading**. *See also* **feminist stylistics**, and Text 19. [70]

semantics The study of meaning as encoded in a language, in abstraction from its use in a particular **context**: cf. **pragmatics**. [19]

sentence adverb Textual element (e.g. *perhaps, probably, undoubtedly*) expressing the **modality** of a whole sentence or clause, and conveying the attitude of the speaker towards what he or she is claiming, e.g. *Undoubtedly, political and economic factors have played their part*: *See* **ideological perspective**. [39]

stream of consciousness technique A style of representation of thought which appears to be the freest form of **direct thought** (**DT**) and creates the illusion that, without narrator interference, readers have direct access to the random flow of thought of characters, i.e. to their inner **points of view**. This technique is also known as **interior monologue**. *See* **free indirect discourse** (**FID**). *See also* Text 15. [50]

style in language A set of conscious or unconscious choices of expression, inspired or induced by a particular **context**. *See also* Texts 1–3, and 10. [3]

stylistics The study of style in language, i.e. the analysis of distinctive linguistic expression and the description of its purpose and effect. *See also* Text 1. [4]

text Any piece of language which, in terms of communicative meaning, is complete in itself. It is the observable product of a writer's or speaker's **discourse**, which is the process that created the text. *See also* Text 4. [17]

text type *See* **genre**. [6, 11]

texture Metaphorically, the quality of a piece of literary writing in terms of its specific linguistic features, its choices of style (from the Latin word *textura*, 'weaving'). [55, 61]

time deictics Textual elements such as *now, then, yesterday, next week* which reveal to the listener or reader the temporal **perspective** of the speaker or writer in the **discourse**: cf. **person deictics, place deictics**. [35]

Acknowledgements

The authors and publisher are grateful to the following for permission to reproduce the following extracts from copyright material:

Edward Arnold Limited for an extract from *Studying the Novel: An Introduction* (4th edn.) by Jeremy Hawthorn.

Bantam Books, a division of Random House Inc. for the jacket copy from *Dancing Girls and Other Stories* by Margaret Atwood.

Guy Cook for an extract from *Discourse and Literature* © Guy Cook (Oxford University Press 1994).

Faber and Faber Limited for extracts from *An Artist of the Floating World* by Kazuo Ishiguro; 'Clearances' from *The Haw Lantern* by Seamus Heaney; *The Government of the Tongue* by Seamus Heaney; 'The Trees' from *Collected Poems* by Philip Larkin.

Heinle & Heinle, a division of Thomson Learning for extracts from *Aspects of Language* (3rd edn.) by Dwight Bolinger © (1981); *Linguistics for Students of Literature* (1st edn.) by Elizabeth Closs Traugott and Mary Louise Pratt © (1980).

Macmillan for 'Philip Larkin and Symbolism' by Andrew Motion, in *Philip Larkin*, edited by Stephen Regan.

Macmillan Education Ltd., reproduced by permission of Palgrave, for an extract from *The Language of James Joyce* by Katie Wales © Katie Wales (1992).

John Murray Publishers Limited for 'Devonshire Street, W1' from *Collected Poems* by John Betjeman.

Pearson Education Limited for extracts from *Style in Fiction* by Geoffrey Leech and Michael Short © Longman Group Limited (1981); 'Dialogue in the public sphere' by Norman Fairclough in *Discourse and Social Life* edited by Srikant Sarangi and Malcolm Coulthard © Pearson Education Limited (2000); *A Dictionary of Stylistics* by Katie Wales © Pearson Education Limited (1990, 2001).

Routledge for extracts from *Narrative: A Critical Linguistic Introduction* (2nd edn.) by Michael Toolan; 'Literature and Language' by Mick Short, in *Encyclopedia of Literature and Criticism* edited by M. Coyle, P. Garside, M. Kelsall, and J. Peck; *Feminist Stylistics* by Sara Mills © Sara Mills (1995); *Style and Stylistics* by Graham Hough; *Keywords in Language and Literacy* by Ronald Carter.

Routledge (Unwin Hyman) for an extract from *Language, Discourse and Literature: An Introductory Reader in Discourse Stylistics* edited by Ronald Carter and Paul Simpson.

Routledge (Methuen) for an extract from *Narrative Fiction: Contemporary Poetics* by Shlomith Rimmon-Kenan.

The Estate of James Joyce © Copyright, the Estate of James Joyce, for extracts from *Ulysses* [OUP World's Classics edition 1998].

The Random House Group Limited for an extract from 'Hills Like White Elephants' from *The First Forty Nine Stories* by Ernest Hemingway published by Jonathan Cape.

The Society of Authors as the Literary Representative of the Estate of Virginia Woolf for an extract from *Mrs Dalloway* by Virginia Woolf.

Peter Verdonk for 'The liberation of the icon' from the *Journal of Literary Studies* Volume 15 Number (3/4) December (1999).

H. G. Widdowson for an extract from *Practical Stylistics: An Approach to Poetry* © H. G. Widdowson (Oxford University Press 1992).

Despite every effort to trace and contact copyright holders before publication, this has not always been possible. If notified, the publisher will be pleased to rectify any errors or omissions at the earliest opportunity.

DATE DUE

The Library Store   #47-0106